"MY DEAR WATSON"
BERNARD SHAW'S LETTERS TO A CRITIC

Edited by
L.W. Conolly

The Academy of the Shaw Festival

Distributed by Rock's Mills Press

The original edition of this book included the following Library and Archives Canada Cataloguing in Publication information:

Shaw, Bernard, 1856-1950, author
    "My dear Watson" : Bernard Shaw's letters to a critic
/ edited by L.W. Conolly.

Includes bibliographical references and index.
ISBN 978-1-77506-320-9 (softcover)

    1. Shaw, Bernard, 1856-1950--Correspondence. 2. Watson, Malcolm, 1853-1929--Correspondence. 3. Dramatists, Irish--20th century—Correspondence. 4. Theatre--England--London--Reviews. 5. Theatre--England--London--History--20th century. 6. Theatre critics--England--London--History--20th century. I. Conolly, L. W. (Leonard W.), editor II. Watson, Malcolm, 1853-1929, author III. Academy of the Shaw Festival, issuing body IV. Title.

PR5366.A4848 2017   822'.912   C2017-905130-X

Published in 2017 by
The Academy of the Shaw Festival
P.O. Box 774
Niagara-on-the-Lake, Ontario L0S 1J0
www.shawfest.com

Copyright © 2017 L.W. Conolly
The letters of Bernard Shaw are © 2017 the Estate of Bernard Shaw and are published by kind permission of the Society of Authors on behalf of the Shaw Estate.

No part of this publication may be reproduced or stored in a retrieval system, or transmitted in any form or by any means, electronic, mechanical, recording, or otherwise, without written permission of the publisher.

Designed by Aldo Fierro
Cover photo: George Bernard Shaw, Irish dramatist and critic, 1856 to 1950, at his Ayot St Lawrence home in 1946. Pictorial Press Ltd / Alamy Stock Photo

This edition distributed by Rock's Mills Press.
For information, visit us at www.rocksmillspress.com or contact us at customer.service@rocksmillspress.com.

"My Dear Watson": Bernard Shaw's Letters to a Critic was first published privately on the occasion of the eighth conference of the International Shaw Society, held in Niagara-on-the-Lake, Ontario, 21-25 July 2017, and is dedicated, with admiration and affection, to Michel Pharand: friend, colleague, Shavian, and editor *sans pareil*.

CONTENTS

Acknowledgements • vii

Note on the Text • ix

Introduction • 1

Notes to the Introduction • 7

The Shaw-Watson Letters • 9

Notes to the Letters • 45

Appendix: Selected *Daily Telegraph* Reviews of Shaw Plays • 53

Sources • 95

Index • 97

ACKNOWLEDGEMENTS

My greatest debt is to David Grapes II* for bringing to my attention the Shaw-Watson letters, held in his extensive private theatre collection, and for granting permission for their publication.

I also very much appreciate the help of Dorothy Hadfield (University of Waterloo) in facilitating access to the electronic archive of the *Daily Telegraph*.

Members of my family have again provided expertise in proofreading (Barbara Conolly), editing (Rebecca Conolly), and design (Aldo Fierro). Once more, molte grazie!

And, for the umpteenth time, I have relied on Michel Pharand to rescue me from embarrassing errors and gaffes. Any that remain are, of course, entirely my own responsibility. My appreciation of Michel's generous support and friendship over many years is expressed, however inadequately, in the dedication to this book.

The letters of Bernard Shaw are © 2017 the Estate of Bernard Shaw and are published by kind permission of the Society of Authors on behalf of the Shaw Estate.

All editorial matter is © 2017 L.W. Conolly.

*Currently Professor of Theater and Founding Director of the School of Theater Arts and Dance at the University of Northern Colorado, where he also serves as the Producing Artistic Director for UNC's professional summer stock company (the Little Theater of the Rockies, founded in 1934), David Grapes has combined a distinguished career as a university teacher and administrator with award-winning professional accomplishments as director, actor, drama critic, and playwright. He has provided artistic leadership and has directed and acted at major regional theatres across the United States, is creator or co-creator of several musical reviews and plays that have enjoyed national and international success, and for several years has reviewed plays at the Shaw and Stratford Festivals for the Booth newspaper chain (Michigan), in print for other media outlets, and for his own online Canadian Theatre Festivals BLOG. David Grapes began collecting theatre materials in 1976, since when he has accumulated a rich research and teaching resource, with a particular emphasis on Bernard Shaw and his contemporaries. Holdings in the collection include correspondence, cabinet cards, signed photographs, first editions, programmes, recordings, scripts, ephemera, and memorabilia.

NOTE ON THE TEXT

In Shaw's letters: all titles of plays and novels have been italicized; original spelling (e.g., shew, Shakespere) has been retained; Shaw's punctuation practice after salutations (comma in typed letters, no punctuation in handwritten letters) has been retained; Shaw's often inconsistent practice with apostrophes (don't/dont) has been standardized into current practice; editorial annotations and explanatory notes have been provided.

In *Daily Telegraph* printed materials: all titles of plays and novels have been italicized; obvious typographical errors have been silently corrected; editorial annotations and explanatory notes have been provided in materials directly associated with Shaw's letters, but not in the Appendix, which has, however, been indexed.

The following abbreviations have been used:

ALS   Autograph letter or letter-card signed
ANS   Autograph note on "Compliments" card signed
APCS Autograph postal card signed
HD   Holograph draft
TD   Typed draft
TLS   Typed letter signed

INTRODUCTION

By the time Clement Scott (1841-1904) resigned his position as drama critic of the *Daily Telegraph* at the end of 1897—having held the position since 1871—he had become London theatre's most prominent and influential critic. He had not left the *Telegraph* entirely voluntarily, having compromised his position by publicly expressing the view that the acting profession was a natural and inevitable cause of immorality among actresses. Still, losing Scott was a blow to the *Telegraph*, his unflagging defence of Victorian theatrical verities (as represented principally by Henry Irving) and his acerbic attacks on threats to those values (as represented by the likes of Ibsen and Shaw) having made his columns and reviews obligatory reading among most London theatregoers. Who could possibly fill his shoes?

The natural successor was a man named William Leonard Courtney (1850-1928), already on the *Telegraph* staff, which he had joined in 1890 after stints as an Oxford don and a writer for *The World* and other journals. Courtney was to stay with the *Telegraph* until 1925, as drama critic, literary editor, and leader writer. He was also a playwright, his first play, *Kit Marlowe*, having appeared at the Shaftesbury Theatre on 4 July 1890 (Nicoll, *History of English Drama* 326), and an author of philosophy and other books. One of them, *Old Saws and Modern Instances* (1918), captures his knowledge of Shaw and modern drama generally, and reveals a more welcoming attitude towards new dramatic forms than Scott had ever displayed, while still insisting on strong conservative values. To be as "didactic" as Shaw was, Courtney wrote, is "to miss something of the artist's serenity and to injure the dramatic effect by a constant uplifting of the schoolmaster's forefinger. We go to the drama to listen and think and be silent: we do not cherish the prospect of being soundly birched" (3).

Courtney, however, was a busy man. In addition to his drama and literary responsibilities at the *Telegraph* and his playwriting interests, he took on the editorship of the *Fortnightly Review* in 1894, a position he held until his death, and he also served as Chairman of the publishing house Chapman and Hall (who published a selection of his plays, *Dramas and Diversions*, in 1908). Given his upper crust background (the son of a senior civil servant) and Oxford pedigree, he may also have felt that Scott's weekly theatre column in the *Telegraph*, "Drama of the Day" (a giddy blend of information, speculation, and gossip), was somewhat beneath his dignity.

Enter Malcolm Watson. Unlike Courtney, Watson's family background was not a springboard to Oxford and the best London clubs, and his accomplishments as a playwright and journalist have not earned him recognition in standard reference sources such as the *Oxford Dictionary of National Biography* (and not even a Wikipedia entry). What little information about Watson exists is found in newspaper obituaries, particularly in the *Telegraph* and *The Times*. Surprisingly, *The Times* gave a more detailed account of Watson's life than the *Telegraph* (both obituaries appeared on 8 August 1929, a day after Watson's death).

Born in Glasgow in 1853, the son of a theatre-disapproving doctor, Watson had a sound secondary education at the Glasgow High School, but did not go on to one of Scotland's several universities. Despite his father's objections, Watson developed a taste for theatre, but since his father insisted that his son always be home by 10:00 pm Watson generally missed the last act of every play he saw. After completing his formal education, Watson moved to London to work in a business office, and then to Paris, where he became fluent in French and also took Spanish lessons. His language skills helped him win a position in a London-based Spanish bank, which gave him the income to indulge in London theatregoing (with no parental curfew to worry about) and to try his own hand at playwriting.

Watson submitted one of his early efforts, a comedy called *By Special Request*, to Clement Scott, on whose recommendation it was accepted for production at the Strand Theatre, where it opened on 7 February 1887. Watson went on to write another thirty or so theatre pieces in an eclectic array of genres, from burlesques to serious dramas. One of his burlesques, *Sheerluck Jones, or, Why D'Gillette Him Off* (written with Edward La Serre) ran for 138 performances at Terry's Theatre in 1901 (Wearing, *The London Stage 1900-1909* 1:207), while his earlier full-length drama, *The Pharisee*, ran for almost 100 nights after opening at the Shaftesbury Theatre on 17 November 1890 (*The Times*, 8 August 1929, and Nicoll, *A History of English Drama 1660-1900*, 616). Watson also enjoyed success with musical sketches written for the German Reed Company, which specialized in family entertainment in small London venues for some forty years (1855-95). (A full list of Watson's plays is in Nicoll, *A History of English Drama 1660-1900*, 616, and Nicoll, *English Drama 1900-1930*, 1016.)

According to *The Times*'s obituary, Clement Scott was again influential in Watson's life when he advised him to give up his business career in favour of journalism, whereupon, presumably on Scott's recommendation, he was offered a position with the *St James's Gazette*. For that journal, says *The Times*, Watson "did all sorts of work... special articles, short stories, topical verse, and so forth." The breakthrough into dramatic criticism came on the retirement of the *Gazette*'s critic, Ernest Bendall, either in 1889 (*The Times*) or August 1888 (Kent 36; Kent also indicates that Bendall moved to the *Daily Mail* as that paper's drama critic). Whatever the precise timing, Watson was appointed to succeed Bendall at the *Gazette*, and held the post for the next decade. Then, early in 1899, Watson joined William Courtney at the *Daily Telegraph*.

It seems, however, that the *Telegraph* still felt understaffed for its drama coverage, so another appointment was made. Like Courtney, Henry Christopher Bailey (1878-1961) was an Oxford-educated classical scholar, but he also published his first novel while at Oxford—a historical novel called *My Lady of Orange*. This was the first of some sixty books he wrote, most of them historical fiction and (later in his career) detective fiction (one of his detectives was memorably named Joshua Clunk). Possibly because of an Oxford connection with Courtney, Bailey joined the *Telegraph* in 1901 with little or no previous journalism experience (Davis 160). He remained with the *Telegraph* until 1946, having served as drama critic, war correspondent, and leader writer (*The Times*, 27 March 1961).

Thus, when Bailey joined the *Telegraph* in 1901 the drama team consisted of (in order of appointment and seniority) William Leonard Courtney, Malcolm Watson, and Henry Christopher Bailey. In common with other major British newspapers at the time, drama reviews and columns did not carry a byline, so it is not easy to determine who on the *Telegraph* team wrote what. We do know, however, from his *Telegraph* obituary that Watson was hired specifically to take over Clement Scott's "Drama of the Day" column, which, between Scott's retirement and Watson's appointment, had presumably been Courtney's responsibility.

Scott's specific remit when he joined the *Telegraph* is confirmed by the previously unpublished letters from Shaw to Watson in this edition, the first dated 7 February 1899, the last 18 December 1928. Only fourteen letters from Shaw to Watson from that period have so far come to light—and none from Watson to Shaw. The letters reveal, however, Watson's unflagging pursuit of Shaw for information and insight into his plays and into the theatrical environment that Shaw sought to reform for all of his career. Shaw was an invaluable source for Watson, but Watson was equally valuable to Shaw in providing a direct and unmediated conduit to the public through his "Drama of the Day" and other columns in the *Telegraph*.

How this collaboration worked is evident from Shaw's very first letter to Watson. Watson sought information from Shaw about production plans for *Caesar and Cleopatra*. Shaw immediately provided it. Two days later the information was published in the *Telegraph*. From Shaw's point of view, the process became even more effective when, rather than agreeing to a meeting with Watson to discuss a new play or broader theatrical issues, Shaw simply provided him with a self-drafted interview—questions as well as answers—which Watson then printed in the *Telegraph*. The first instance of this in Shaw's relationship with Watson occurred on 18 October 1905 (Letter 3) about the production of *Major Barbara* at the Royal Court Theatre. This was not the first time that Shaw had drafted an interview for the press,[1] but Shaw's exchanges with Malcolm Watson demonstrate exactly how Shaw and journalists colluded in duping readers into believing they were getting independent reporting when they were really getting, virtually *verbatim*, just what Shaw wanted them to read.[2] Soon dissatisfied, however, with simply reproducing the interview text written by Shaw, Watson began adding rhetorical embroidery (he was, after all, a playwright) to enhance the deception (see Letters 4, 7, 11).

These letters from Shaw to Watson, then, are significant for the light they shed on the working relationship between Shaw and one of London's major newspapers. The letters—and, of course, the "interviews"—also have their own intrinsically interesting subject matter, not least, perhaps, Shaw's views on his own plays: a familiar mix of seriousness, whimsy, orneriness, provocation, and obfuscation. The Shaw-Watson relationship also encompasses important theatrical initiatives, such as the Vedrenne-Barker years at the Royal Court Theatre, the "Afternoon Theatre" matinées at Beerbohm Tree's His Majesty's Theatre in 1909, and Charles Frohman's subsequent (and short-lived) efforts to run a repertory system at the Duke of York's Theatre in 1910. Shaw's attempts to educate Watson on theatre censorship (Letters 5 and 6) add new dimensions to Shaw's deep engagement with the controversial issue, while Watson's "interview" with Shaw (8 April 1914) about anticipated raucous audience behaviour at the opening night of *Pygmalion*, and Shaw's subsequent thank-you to Watson (Letter 12) for his cooperation in trying to establish a "new code of manners in the theatre," speak to Shaw's serious concern about giving actors a fair hearing.

All but one of the letters deal with theatrical matters. The exception (Letter 10) deals with a personal income tax question that Watson had raised with Shaw. Apart from revealing Shaw's knowledge of British tax legislation, the letter suggests that the professional relationship between the two men had reached a level of comfort and respect that enabled such discussion of personal matters.

Shaw's letters to Watson, and the self-drafted interviews that accompanied some of the letters, provide the backbone of the narrative of their relationship over a period of nearly thirty years. The absence of Watson's letters to Shaw, together with lengthy gaps (one of twelve years) in Shaw's letters to Watson, necessarily make it a fractured narrative. I have provided relevant context to link the letters, including transcripts of Watson's columns on Shaw in cases where correspondence concerning them has not yet come to light.

In the Appendix (p. 53) I have given full transcripts of, or lengthy extracts from, *Daily Telegraph* reviews of Shaw's major plays during the years that Watson worked for the paper. Only one of these has previously been reprinted (*Heartbreak House*, in Evans 246-48), so it seems worthwhile for their own sake to include them here. In so far as the *Daily Telegraph* represented the values of its theatregoing readers, we get a good sense from the reviews of thoughtful but generally conservative opinions of Shaw's plays: no Clement Scott–like rhetorical rampaging against the unfamiliar and the challenging, but no fervent embracing, either. Shaw, the *Telegraph* allowed, could not be measured "by the ordinary standards that prevail in the theatre" (*You Never Can Tell*). Was he even writing what could be called "plays"? *John Bull's Other Island*, for example, "was no play, and never intended to be one." *Getting Married* could more properly be called a "Socratic dialogue" than a play, and *Misalliance* was really just "a conversation," whose characters are "talking machines." Or, in *Heartbreak House*, "puppets." And what in any case does it all *mean*? In *Major Barbara* "the meaning is that there is no meaning." Put another way, in *Pygmalion* "you never get anywhere, you do not much want to get anywhere"—but there is some consolation in that "you meet plenty of good things on the way." Yes, "as a reformer of our politics and our morality he is in more deadly earnest than our most advanced politicians" (*Caesar and Cleopatra*), but those ubiquitous Shavian paradoxes are confusing, and his prolixity makes for long, long evenings in the theatre. But, perhaps in spite of himself, he does get it right sometimes. The "remarkable and significant" *Doctor's Dilemma* has marks of "a real play," with "firmness and decision in Mr Shaw's characterisation, and a greater attention than it is his wont to pay to the process of construction." And for once he even manages in that play to introduce some "genuine tenderness" and, in Jennifer Dubedat, a "loving woman." *Saint Joan* is also "a remarkable piece of work," while in *Androcles and the Lion* the laughter, often inconsequential in Shaw's plays, generates "qualms of conscience." And is it "good fortune" or the "admirable skill" of "the Bernard Shaw theatre" that "bring[s] out all the best that there is in the actors and actresses who interpret it"?

Who on the *Telegraph*'s drama staff—Courtney, Watson, Bailey—wrote what, we do not know. It is unlikely that Watson would have displaced Courtney before establishing himself with the paper, and even less likely that the inexperienced Bailey would have been assigned to review major productions. But given Courtney's other interests and responsibilities, it seems reasonable to assume that the very experienced Watson would eventually have begun to share the role of *Telegraph* drama critic with Courtney. In its obituary of Watson, *The Times* takes it even further, stating that after a stint as drama columnist *and* critic at the short-lived *Sunday Telegraph*[3] Watson was assigned the same responsibilities at the daily edition. It was his *Telegraph* work that cemented his reputation, as assessed by *The Times*, as "a critic of ripe experience and discernment, whose judgments were valuable to dramatic art as well as to contemporary newspaper-readers." We are fortunate that Shaw's letters to Watson provide some substance to a hitherto unacknowledged relationship.

NOTES TO THE INTRODUCTION

1 Evans, 4, identifies Shaw's first self-drafted interview as a piece on *Widowers' Houses*, published in *The Star* on 29 November 1892 (C907 in Laurence, *Bibliography*).
2 Shaw's annoyance when pre-production information leaked out about his plays can be seen in his complaint to the editor of the *Daily Express* when Malcolm Watson's colleague at that paper, Archibald Haddon, used his "Green Room Gossip" column on 14 November 1906 to disclose unauthorized information about *The Doctor's Dilemma* (Laurence, *Theatrics* 75-76). "Some wretch in the theatre has just given away the whole plot & some of the dialogue to the Express," Shaw told William Archer (Laurence, *Collected Letters* 2:659). See also Letter 4, below.
3 A different paper from the *Sunday Telegraph* launched in 1961 and still being published. The dates of the earlier imprint are unknown. One wonders as well if the critic who praised Shaw in the *Telegraph* review of *The Doctor's Dilemma* for creating (in Jennifer Dubedat) "a loving woman" who "loves her husband with [an] unreasoning affection," lifting her "into a wholly new category of Mr Shaw's women" (below, p. 64), could also subsequently have criticized him for never having written "a love scene which was worth listening to" (Courtney, *The Passing Hour* 245).

THE SHAW-WATSON LETTERS

The opening sentence of the first extant Shaw letter to Malcolm Watson indicates that the letter was written in response to Watson having introduced himself to Shaw—not at that time an established West End playwright—shortly after his appointment as theatre critic of the Daily Telegraph *early in 1899. In support of the inauguration of what would prove to be a mutually beneficial collaboration over many years, Shaw provided Watson with information about delays in the production of* Caesar and Cleopatra, *which Shaw had completed in December 1898.*

1. [ALS]

Blen-Cathra
Hindhead
Haslemere
Surrey[1]

7 February 1899

P R I V A T E !!!!!!

Dear Watson

I congratulate the D.T. [*Daily Telegraph*]; and I shall of course be only too glad to advertise myself in your column whenever you will let me. But you know what theatrical business is—all project and very little come-off. *Caesar and Cleopatra* is an accomplished fact. The play is written and ready; and if you will find a theatre and ten thousand pounds for Forbes Robertson you may announce its production for next winter. I am agreeable; F.R. is agreeable; Mrs P.C. is agreeable.[2] But a magnificent spectacular historical play in five acts, with nine scenes, thirty[-]four costumed characters, and Roman armies and Egyptian courts <u>ad lib</u>, takes some backing: it cannot, as you may guess, be done on the profits of *Macbeth*.[3] I have promised not to dispose of the play in any other quarter until F.R. has had time to rally his forces (not, that is, before May) so that there is no danger of a summer production—indeed I should object to that anyhow, as the hot weather spoils a summer run and the stampede at the end of the season limits it. But F.R. may be forced back on a cheaper play; he may fail to get a suitable theatre; a dozen things may happen to upset the applecart. All that can be safely said at present is that the miserable equipment of most of our London theatres in the way of stage room and stage machinery places great difficulty in the way of producing pieces on the scale of C & C, and that all announcements are premature until F.R. has found a home for his next enterprise. You will have to use your discretion in devising what to say & how to say it: the above is the private truth of the situation, which may be summed up in the statement that as things stand at present F.R. will only be too jolly glad to produce the play if it runs to it.

However, if one cannot publicly print sense about it, one can print nonsense. For example, you can say that the play has been written to redeem English dramatic literature from the reproach of having no better portrait of Julius Caesar than the wretched abortion produced by Shakespere. His Cleopatra, too, though a very clever dramatization of the ordinary demirep,[4] does not touch on the only really interesting event in her career, her meeting with Caesar.

I must break off now to catch the post. I shall soon send you some printed particulars as to the names of the characters &c. If there is anything special you want to know, ask me.

I am greatly crippled by the hole in my foot;[5] but it is nothing alarming, only one of those long sinuses which take such a devil of a time to heal. The golden rule as to the conflicting reports about my health is: don't believe any of them.

Yrs ever
G. Bernard Shaw

Without much regard for Shaw's caution that his letter was private, but taking full advantage of Shaw's granting him "discretion" in how to use it, Watson quickly published information from it, with direct quotes, in his regular "Drama of the Day" column in the Telegraph *on 9 February 1899, adding only that he hoped that Shaw's admonition of Shakespeare's take on Cleopatra "will not be taken too seriously by a matter-of-fact and prosaically-minded public." The British (and American) public weren't able to decide how seriously to take anything about the play until it was published in* Three Plays for Puritans *(with* The Devil's Disciple *and* Captain Brassbound's Conversion*) in both London and New York in 1901—unless, that is, they were lucky enough to get to the copyright reading in Newcastle on 15 March 1899. London audiences had to wait to form an opinion* until the play's première at the Savoy Theatre on 25 November 1907, reviewed in the Telegraph *on 26 November 1907 (see Appendix, p. 70). The first American professional production of* Caesar and Cleopatra *was at the New Amsterdam Theatre in New York on 30 October 1906.*

There is a gap of more than five years before the next extant letter from Shaw to Watson. During that time Watson had continued to write about Shaw in "Drama of the Day" *and the* Telegraph *continued to review his plays, which by now were becoming an important presence at the Royal Court Theatre under the management of Harley Granville Barker and John Vedrenne (see, for example, reviews of* John Bull's Other Island *and* Man and Superman, *Appendix, pp. 55, 57).*[6]

But Watson's interest was also aroused by a less prominent Shaw production in an unconventional performance venue. He contacted Shaw about his "brief tragedy" (Shaw's phrase) with a tantalising title: Passion, Poison, and Petrifaction, or The Fatal Gazogene. *Shaw wrote this for performance at a garden party on 14 July 1905 at London's Royal Botanical Gardens in aid of the Actors' Orphanage Fund. Shaw was again forthcoming in his response to Watson.*

2. [ALS]

10 Adelphi Terrace, W.C.

3 July 1905

[No salutation]

I really know nothing about the Orphanage affair except about a tenth of what Miss Warley[7] knows. The play contains many profound truths and vivid flashes of characterization touching the police and public question, the medical profession, the marriage question, the fashionable clothes question, the craze for fine art, the influence of dramatic critics on modern plays, the probable character of the music sung in heaven, the land question in towns, the drink question, the mineral water question, the servant question, and the question of first aid to the poisoned. This is of course much less than my usual allowance of subjects; but the limitation to 12 minutes made it impossible for me to cover as much ground as in my Court Theatre pieces. Still, there is much food for thought in the little piece; and the more earnest section of my disciples should make a point of seeing it several times in succession at the Botanic Gardens.

G.B.S.

Watson promoted Passion *in "Drama of the Day" on 6 July 1905 by quoting Shaw's comments in full (except for the reference to Miss Warley), and the* Telegraph *carried a brief, non-judgemental account of the whimsical action and characters of the play on 15 July 1905.*

Meanwhile, news was circulating about a new Shaw play at the Royal Court. Watson, it seems, had approached John Vedrenne to find out more about it. Vedrenne mentioned this to Shaw, who obligingly "scribbled off a bit of an interview" and sent it to Watson. This was the first of the self-drafted interviews that Shaw provided to Watson. The play was Major Barbara.

3. [ALS]

10 Adelphi Terrace, W.C.

18 October 1905

Dear Malcolm Watson

Vedrenne tells me you want something about my new play. It is quite indescribable, as there is no plot or sensation of the ordinary kind in it. I have scribbled off a bit of an interview—it is all I can think of & will save you the trouble of compiling a paragraph. In haste, which pray excuse.

ever
G. Bernard Shaw.

[TD]

M.W.   What about the new play?
G.B.S.   Oh, please don't call it a play. There was a general agreement that *John Bull's Other Island* was not a play; and it has been a success on that understanding. If you put it about that *Major Barbara* is a play, nobody will come to it. I assure you it is much less of a play than *John Bull*.
M.W.   May one call it a tragedy or a comedy or a farce or what is called in the theatre a drama?
G.B.S.   No: it is simply a discussion in four very long acts; and that is what it will be called on the playbill.
M.W.   I see. A problem play.
G.B.S.   Great Heavens! don't call it that. About fifteen years ago for some inscrutable reason London made up its mind that a problem play meant a cut-and-dried play about an improper female. I pledge you my word every

	woman in *Major Barbara* goes right through the play without a stain on her character. There is no drama, no situations, no curtains, no feeling, no heart, no dramatic interest: in one word, no adultery.
M.W.	You consider that the improper female should not be allowed on the stage, do you?
G.B.S.	Certainly not. Do you forget that I am the author of three unpleasant plays?[8] But really I cannot shut my eyes to the fact that there are other and much more interesting people in the world than the improper female and her husband and her lover, just as there are other figures in history besides Lady Hamilton and Mary queen o' Scots.[9] And then consider the almost insuperable difficulty of getting such people credibly represented on the stage. Is there any spectacle more absurd than a respectable, industrious, accomplished lady—a leading London actress in short—desperately pretending to be no better than she ought to be. Mr Pinero has made one or two remarkable dramatic studies of unfortunate females;[10] and what has been the result on stage? First, a representation of Mrs Patrick Campbell cut by the county when she would obviously have had it at her feet in a fortnight. Second, Miss Fay Davis[11] being talked at through a whole evening as an abandoned person when a bishop could have married her without hesitation at the end of every act. There is only one imposture more transparent than the poor castaway in the police court pretending to be an actress; and that is the eminent actress on the west end stage pretending to be a castaway. Impropriety is no use on the stage: you can't get it acted.
M.W.	Yes; but to return to *Major Barbara*—
G.B.S.	Oh, I've told you all about it. There's really nothing more to be said.
M.W.	You have told me nothing about it. Is it true that you are going to burlesque the Salvation Army?
G.B.S.	My dear Watson, do you suppose that I, who have so often stood preaching my gospel on the kerbstone at one corner of the street while the Salvation lass preached hers at the opposite corner, am going to revive the stale blackguardisms of the forgotten Skeleton Army at her expense? I never burlesque anything: on the contrary it is my business to find some order and meaning in the apparently insane farce of life as it happens higgledy-higgledy-piggledy off the stage. No: I shall give the devil as fair play as I give General Booth;[12] and I shall not hesitate to put my finger on the weak spots in Salvationism; but as against the fashionable world I also am a street corner man and a Salvationist; and you may depend on it I shall play for my side.
M.W.	It has been reported that there is a scene with a prizefighter[13]—

G.B.S. All nonsense. No prizefighter appears in the play. No fight occurs on the stage. I tell you again nothing happens in the play except to people's souls. They all preach right through. Make that fact public for me, or we shall have all the free lists in London coming and demanding seats. I repeat, it isn't what they call a play. And now I must be off, as the prompt copy is not yet ready for the typist. Goodbye; and may you be there to see.

Watson lost no time in getting this "interview" into the Telegraph *(next day, 19 October).*[14] *The information, he proudly claimed, was "extorted at the sword's point, at a reluctantly accorded interview." And while "considerations of space," he said, necessitated the omission of the "interviewer's" questions, for the most part he neatly incorporated Shaw's questions into Shaw's answers. As Shaw had hoped, Watson attended the première of Major Barbara at the Royal Court on 28 November 1905. The* Telegraph *review is given below (p. 59).*

Watson was also very probably at the Royal Court on 20 March 1906 to see Captain Brassbound's Conversion (see the Telegraph *review, Appendix, p. 62), and then his attention turned to another forthcoming Shaw play, again at the Court—The Doctor's Dilemma. Perhaps disgruntled that he was missing out on stories about the play that were circulating in the press, he contacted Shaw, and, in response, Shaw sent Watson another self-drafted interview. The original ("the enclosed") has been lost, but we can learn (with some confidence) what was in it because Watson published it in the* Telegraph *on 11 October 1906, again without any indication that he had not actually interviewed Shaw. Indeed, the deception this time was enhanced by Watson's adding histrionic touches of seeming authenticity ("Upon the last three words Mr Shaw lingered with a tender air of regret . . . . With an audible sigh of relief, Mr Shaw despatched his visitor"). The* Telegraph *review of* The Doctor's Dilemma *appeared on 21 November 1906 (Appendix, p. 63).*

4. [ALS]

10 Adelphi Terrace, W.C.

10 October 1906

Dear Malcolm Watson

The cat is so completely out of the bag about *The Doctor's Dilemma* that there is nothing more to be said about it short of giving away the whole story of the play

& spoiling its reception. I had to give Archer all that I <u>could</u> give beforehand, for obvious reasons.[15] But the enclosed will serve your turn & save you the trouble of compiling a paragraph.

Yrs ever
G. Bernard Shaw

Watson's "interview" on The Doctor's Dilemma, Daily Telegraph,
11 October 1906.[16]

To interview Mr Bernard Shaw is at once the easiest and most difficult thing in the world. He will talk on every subject except the one immediately in hand, while his opinions regarding his own and others' work are of so daring a kind as almost to baffle reproductions. Invited yesterday to give some particulars regarding his new play, *The Doctor's Dilemma*, he replied, with charming and emphatic inconsequence, that *The Silver Box* (Mr John Galsworthy's play now being performed at the Court) was a first-rate dramatic work.[17] Messrs Vedrenne and Barker, he hurriedly added, are really creating dramatic literature. Fortunately, the admission led apparently—or may we suggest naturally?—to a different train of thought, with *The Doctor's Dilemma* as the final goal. "I fear," said Mr Shaw, somewhat wistfully, "the title will have to be changed, as it has already been used in the case of a novel by Miss Hesba Stretton, authoress of *Jessica's First Prayer*."[18] Upon the last three words Mr Shaw lingered with a tender air of regret. It seemed almost as if he grudged their ownership to the lady in question.

Presently, however, he allowed himself to be coaxed back to the subject of *The Doctor's Dilemma*. "It is a cheap job," he stated, rather pathetically. "Anybody can write a play about births, marriages, and deaths, just as anyone can write a novel about a mother or a dying child. The truth is, William Archer has started me on an enterprise utterly unworthy of my powers. So far from death being the supreme test of an author's ability, it is the crutch of every dramatic cripple, the onion of every actor who cannot pump up a real tear. Life is the important thing; who cares how, when, or where anybody dies? I am going to die myself one of these days; why don't you interview me about that if it is so enormously interesting and important?"

"A baby in arms could have written this play of mine as far as the death part of it is concerned. Pathos? Oh, yes, there will be lots of pathos; the Court Theatre will be damp with tears and windy with sniffs; the fourth act will give London rheumatism. The really difficult and interesting part is the handling of that pressing modern problem, the doctor—the man who has a pecuniary interest in mutilation and an absolute license to commit murder. That is what sensible people will come to hear. They will have to bring their brains with them, too. The first act is like 150 pages out of Joyce's *Scientific Dialogues* [1807].[19] Did you ever hear of Opsonin? Of course not; you spend your life in the theatre, and therefore never hear of anything that is going on in the world. Well, *The Doctor's Dilemma* is all about Opsonin. So glad to have met you and had the chance of telling you all about it. Good-bye." And with an audible sigh of relief, Mr Shaw despatched his visitor.

In the three years before Shaw's next extant letter to Watson, the Telegraph *did not neglect Shaw. The paper reviewed* The Philanderer *at the Court on 6 February 1907 ("If* The Philanderer *proves anything it is that the Ibsenites were rather silly and the older generation quite sane"—a remark that Clement Scott would have heartily endorsed), and Watson (and/or one of his colleagues) spent another mostly unsatisfying afternoon at the Court on 4 June 1907 seeing performances of* Don Juan in Hell *("a long rambling philosophical treatise . . . a debate or sermon rather than a play") and* The Man of Destiny *(if "judiciously cut" it would be "an admirable curtain-raiser"). Then the* Telegraph *was at the Savoy Theatre for the London premières of* The Devil's Disciple *and* Caesar and Cleopatra *(14 October 1907 and 25 November 1907, respectively; see Appendix, pp. 68 and 70 for reviews), and when the opening of* Getting Married *(Haymarket Theatre 12 May 1908) approached, Watson was again keen to get some inside information about the play from Shaw. The correspondence with Shaw about* Getting Married *has not survived, but judging from what Watson printed in the* Telegraph *a few days before the play's opening, it is clear that Shaw again provided him with the script of an "interview." "I have promised Watson first bite," Shaw told Vedrenne (Laurence,* Collected Letters *2:771).*

Watson's "interview" with Shaw on Getting Married, Daily Telegraph, *7 May 1908*[20]

MR BERNARD SHAW ON HIS NEW PLAY

Yesterday (writes a representative of *The Daily Telegraph* [i.e., Watson]) I claimed from Mr Bernard Shaw the fulfilment of an old promise that he would tell me something about his new play over and above what has to be told to everybody through the usual official communications. From these it is already known that the piece is entitled *Getting Married*; that it is to be produced at the Haymarket Theatre on the afternoon of the 12th; that it will, in performance, last nearly three hours; that it is in form a perfect Greek play with the unities of time and place strictly preserved; that the action is supposed to take place on the afternoon of the day on which the play is produced, provided the weather is suitable; and that it is neither a tragedy nor a comedy, but simply "an instructive conversation."

"What more can you possibly want to know?" said Mr Shaw, in response to a demand for further particulars.

"Why is Mr Granville Barker not in the cast?"

"Because he is busy writing a new play.[21] However, as there is a general desire that he should be associated with this production, he has consented to understudy the part of the Beadle. He will also produce a new play called *The Chinese Lantern*, by Mr Laurence Housman, whose *Prunella* was one of the Court successes."[22]

"The Vedrenne and Barker enterprise then is as much alive as ever?"

"More so, unfortunately, for Vedrenne and Barker and myself. We honestly did our best to bury it. But it seems to be immortal. We escaped from the Court Theatre only to find ourselves in two theatres—the Savoy and the Queen's. We broke away from them. We announced our death. The news was received with every shade of relief, from polite condolences to open exultation by the Press. Our funeral was duly celebrated, and our miserable end held up as a warning to all pioneers. Yet here we are again, in a still better theatre for our purposes, again staggering under our burden, again longing for the peace of irretrievable ruin, and again unable to achieve it. Let it be a warning to you. It is easier to begin these things than to stop them. We have not only failed to extricate ourselves; we have dragged Mr Frederick Harrison[23] into it. Or perhaps he has dragged us back into it; I hardly know which."

REVENGE ON THE CRITICS

"The attraction of a new play by you must have been irresistible?"

"Not a bit of it. This play is my revenge on the critics for their gross ingratitude to us, their arrant Philistinism, their shameless intellectual laziness, their low tastes, their hatred of good work, their puerile romanticism, their disloyalty to dramatic literature, their stupendous ignorance, their susceptibility to cheap sentiment, their insensibility to honour, virtue, intellectual honesty, and everything that constitutes strength and dignity in human character—in short, for all the vices and follies and weaknesses of which Vedrenne and Barker have been trying to cure them for four years past."

In [the] face of such a cyclonic outburst, what could the overwhelmed interviewer do but murmur a few words of acknowledgment of the unsolicited tribute to the majesty of the Press, and inquire [about] the exact nature of the revenge to be wrought by the new play?

"It is very simple," said Mr Shaw. "You remember *A Dream of Don Juan in Hell*, at the Court.[24] You remember the tortured howl of rage and anguish with which it was received in the Press. Yet that lasted only 110 minutes; and it was made attractive by music and by the magically fascinating stage pictures contrived by Mr Charles Ricketts[25] —a stroke of art which would have made a sensation in any other capital in Europe, and which was here passed over with complete unintelligence. Well, this time the 110 minutes of discussion will be stretched out to 150 minutes. There will be no costumes by Mr Ricketts, nothing but a bishop in an apron. There will be no music by Mr Theodore Stier[26] or Mozart or anyone else. There will be nothing but talk, talk, talk, talk, talk—Shaw talk. The characters will seem to the wretched critics to be simply a row of Shaws, all arguing with one another on totally uninteresting subjects. Shaw in a bishop's apron will argue with Shaw in a general's uniform. Shaw in an alderman's gown will argue with Shaw dressed as a beadle. Shaw dressed as a bridegroom will be wedded to Shaw in petticoats. The whole thing will be hideous, indescribable—an eternity of brain-racking dulness. And yet they will have to sit it out. I see that one or two of them have been trying to cheer themselves with futile guesses at something cheerful to come. They are mistaken; they will suffer—suffer horribly, inhumanly—suffer all the more because when, at last, the final fall of the curtain releases them, and they stagger away to pen their maddened protest, and to assure the public that *Getting Married* is not a play, and not even a bearable experience, they will do so at the risk of being reminded by their editors that they said all this before— said it of *John Bull's Other Island*[27]—said it of *Arms and the Man*, and of *Caesar and Cleopatra*—said it when they had plenty of fun, plenty of scenery, plenty of music, plenty of brilliant costumes; so that now, when their worst terrors have been realised, and all the delights for which they were so grossly ungrateful have been taken away from them, the tale of their suffering will not be believed. Well, serve them right! I am not a vindictive man; but there is such a thing as poetic justice; and on next Tuesday afternoon it will assume its sternest retributive form."

TOUCHES OF MERCY

"Then, will no concessions be made to human weakness?"

"Yes, a few. We shall not be altogether merciless. The curtain will be dropped casually from time to time to allow of first-aid to the really bad cases in the seats allotted to the Press. And Mr Harrison has very kindly arranged with the authorities of the Charing-cross Hospital to have an ambulance available in case of need."

"Am I to understand that in order to revenge yourself on the Press you have deliberately written a bad play?"

"Good heavens, no; there is nothing they would like better. I have deliberately written a good play; that is the way to make the Press suffer. Besides, you will please observe that the enterprise in which we are engaged is not one to be fooled with. My play is the very best I can write; the cast is the very best available in London; and, what is equally important, the audiences will be the best audiences in London. Those audiences will enjoy the play and admire the acting keenly. But if we are to please such audiences, we cannot please everybody. If you turned a Tivoli or London Pavilion audience into the Queen's Hall[28] and inflicted Beethoven's Ninth Symphony on them, they would remember the experience with horror to the end of their lives. That is what is the matter with most of our critics— they are very decent fellows, but they are Tivoli critics, and the Vedrenne and Barker authors are on the Beethovenian plane. Hence, naturally, ructions! We appear to be wantonly mocking and insulting the wrong people, when we are simply doing our best most earnestly to cater for the right people. There is not a single artist concerned in the production who would consent to be made a party to any wanton eccentricity or tomfoolery. The satisfaction of the people for whom we really work will be as keen as the sufferings of the others will be hideous."

THE PLOT

Would it be indiscreet to ask you to lift a corner of the curtain prematurely, and give some notion of the plot of the play?"

"The play has no plot. Surely nobody expects a play by me to have a plot. I am a dramatic poet, not a plotmonger."

"But at least there is a story?"

"Not at all. If you look at any of the old editions of our classical plays, you will see that the description of the play is not called a plot or a story, but an argument. That exactly describes the material of my play. It is an argument—an argument lasting nearly three hours, and carried on with unflagging cerebration by twelve people and a beadle. They are all honourable, decent, nice people. You will find the materials for their argument in the Church Catechism, the Book of Common Prayer, Mr Sidney Webb's letters to the *Times* on the subject of the birth-rate,[29] the various legal text-books on the law of marriage, the sermons and table-talk of the present Bishop of Birmingham and the late Bishop of London (Mandall Creighton),[30] *Whitaker's Almanack*, *The Statesman's Year-Book*, *The Statistical Abstract*, the Registrar-General's returns, and other storehouses of fact and succulent stores of contemporary opinion. All who are intelligent enough to make these their daily reading will have a rare treat; but I am bound to add that people who prefer novelettes will have to pay repeated visits to the play before they acquire a thoroughly unaffected taste for it. If you would like me to go into the subject of the play in detail, I shall be delighted to do so."

"Thank you," said the interviewer, hurriedly, "I am quite satisfied, and space even in *The Daily Telegraph* is limited. I have no doubt we shall have a most enjoyable afternoon on the 12th, although some of us may, as you suggest, have to spend the following day in Charing-cross Hospital. The dramatic critic, of course, is always open to such risks, but in the cause of duty he never refuses to face them. That accounts for the heavy death-rate among them, a fact which so comprehensive an observer of life as yourself cannot have failed to take note; and now it only remains for me to say good-day and to wish all success to *Getting Married*."

The Telegraph *reviewed* Getting Married, *not altogether positively (see Appendix, p. 72), and then, eager to discover Shaw's response to the reviews (especially in the light of his predictions of negative reaction to the play), Watson inveigled out of Shaw another "interview." Again, the original has not survived, but Watson, as usual, placed it in the* Telegraph.

*Watson's post-*Getting Married*"interview" with Shaw,* Daily Telegraph,
14 May 1908[31]

It would have been difficult to find a more contented man than Mr Bernard Shaw yesterday. He had read all, or most of, the notices relating to the production of his new play, *Getting Married*, at the Haymarket, and the delight occasioned by their perusal brought a glow of satisfaction to his face. Praise to the ordinary dramatist is as the very breath of his nostrils; but Mr Shaw, of course, is no ordinary dramatist, and he would rather have the fulfilment of his predictions than a whole volume of eulogistic criticisms. "For once," he exultantly exclaimed, "the critics have come up to my expectations. They have said exactly what I said they would say in respect of *Getting Married*. By their complete unanimity they have absolutely cut the ground from under my feet—how can I possibly take exception to the realisation of my own prophecies? There is one point, however, which I should rather like to insist on. *Getting Married* should never have been criticised by men. It deals with a subject which women only can really understand, and it is lady critics who should have been deputed to pass judgment upon it."

No one familiar with Mr Shaw's dialectic resources will suppose that the above statement exhausted his views on the subject. "To come to facts," he continued, "the general trend of the criticisms upon *Getting Married* seems to be that the first act was both intelligible and amusing, the second somewhat less so, and the last entirely unintelligible and unamusing. Now, the first act was, as it happens, sheer farcical comedy, and consequently easily to be comprehended by the most ordinary understanding. The second was sociological comedy, and naturally more difficult of comprehension. The third, on the other hand, was a compound of pure instinctive poetry and religion. And to how many people, I would ask, do such things make any real appeal; how many have either the desire or the ability to grasp even the significance of the words? For years the critics have complained that my work is all head and no heart, sheer intellect and no feeling. And now that I give them an act compact of poetry and imagination they fall upon and rend me, demanding that I shall explain it logically! Could anything be more unreasonable?" Thus Mr Shaw.

A similar process—i.e., Watson requesting information, Shaw providing the text of an "interview"—occurred with The Admirable Bashville, *which opened at Herbert Beerbohm Tree's His Majesty's Theatre on 26 January 1909 under the auspices of "The Afternoon Theatre," a short-lived series of matinées founded by Tree "for the cultured classes," as Shaw put it.*

This is another instance where the original text of the self-drafted interview has not survived, but we can be sure that Watson's published version (with Watson's usual rhetorical additions) closely followed what Shaw had written for him.

Watson's "interview" with Shaw on The Afternoon Theatre and The Admirable Bashville, Daily Telegraph, *25 January 1909*[32]

THE AFTERNOON THEATRE
MR BERNARD SHAW'S VIEWS

It is not every day that one happens upon Mr Bernard Shaw in a communicative mood. Loquacity with some people is a gift that comes by accident rather than by design; opportunity in such instances is everything. Consequently, finding Mr Shaw prepared to talk about the Afternoon Theatre, and the production to-morrow by that society at His Majesty's of his early play, *The Admirable Bashville*, and of other matters appertaining more or less to the theatre, to Shakespeare, and the musical glasses [sic], the writer seized occasion by the hand, and straightway encouraged him to proceed by putting the following question:

"Are we to infer from your appearance at Mr Tree's theatre that it is all over with Messrs Vedrenne and Barker, the new drama, and all the rest of it?"

"I wish it were," was Mr Shaw's grim reply, "The new drama is like John Barleycorn: you kill it and bury it and go home to your regular work and your peaceful sleep, leaving the critics to guard the grave and lay the ghost with bell, book, and candle, and before you have begun to enjoy your respite the thing is up and alive again, with its wounds closing faster than the critics can inflict them. Vedrenne and Barker is dead—dead after being damned for four years by the London Press; and Mr Vedrenne, Mr Barker, and myself are sitting with all our weight on the coffin, trembling lest the creature should be buried alive after all. We have no assurance that it may not break out at any moment and begin again to work us to death, bringing down the whole London Press on our unfortunate reputations, emptying our pockets, and exhausting our health and strength. I beg you to give every possible publicity to the fact that Vedrenne and Barker is dead, destroyed, ruined; that the passing craze is over; that it is agreed that the Court Theatre plays were not plays at all; that its audiences consisted wholly of unwholesome cranks; that we have all gone back to the daily round, the what-you-may-call-'em task; and that we will see England considerably farther before we again attempt to save her by our private enterprise from the disgrace of having no national theatre. London has nothing more to fear."

HIS MAJESTY'S ALL RIGHT

"But what about His Majesty's Theatre?"

"His Majesty's Theatre is all right. If the Afternoon Theatre empties its exchequer and drives away its frequenters, Mr Tree will come back from Egypt and restore its prosperity. His Majesty's can afford to keep an afternoon theatre for the cultured classes—alias the unwholesome cranks—just as Mr Pierpont Morgan can afford to keep a picture gallery for them in New York.[33] Mr Tree always used to come to the Court Theatre. He was one of the unwholesome cranks. He was quite as regular as Mr Balfour, Sir Oliver Lodge, and Archdeacon Wilberforce, and much more regular than the King, who set the example.[34] It was like going to an opium den; Mr Tree got the habit, and would not be content until he had introduced it at his own theatre. The step was made easy for him by the fact that one of his ablest lieutenants, Mr Frederick Whelen,[35] was a theatrical pioneer of great experience; he had led the enterprise known as the Stage Society, which soon afterwards annexed Mr Granville Barker, and so indirectly brought Vedrenne and Barker into the world."

"The Afternoon Theatre, then, is going to continue the work of Vedrenne and Barker?"

"It will provide a refuge for the homeless and unemployed patrons of Vedrenne and Barker. The plight of these poor people would move a heart of stone. They have acquired the playgoing habit, formerly unknown among intellectually active public-spirited people; and yet they cannot stand the sort of plays that critics like—the plays that really are plays, you know. Of course, they get a *Thunderbolt*, or a Barrie play occasionally at the regular theatres;[36] but Vedrenne and Barker accustomed them to a new play of the most crushing intellectuality and inhuman length every fortnight or so, and they have been miserable ever since. Even some of the critics miss their torture. They want something substantial to damn. You see, people used to read their notices when they had something fresh to write about. I used to read them myself eagerly, as I always judge of the execution I have done by the shrieks of the wounded."

THE THÉÂTRE INTIME

"Don't you find His Majesty's rather large for your plays after the comparative intimacy of the Court stage?"

"On the contrary. I find myself for the first time in the sort of theatre that suits my style. I am no believer in the "théâtre intime." When I was in Stockholm last year I attended the performance of one of the "chamber plays" of that very remarkable genius who was left by Ibsen's death at the head of the Scandinavian drama, as far as European fame is concerned—I mean, of course, August Strindberg.[37] There was a "théâtre intime" for you if you like! It would hardly have made a refreshment-bar for the Criterion Theatre. But the play, though this theatre was built expressly for its performance, would have been much more effective in the Opera House. There are many theatres that are too small for my plays, and hardly any that are large enough."

"But surely His Majesty's stage requires a big production?"

"Not a bit of it. Look at Miss Mack's little chamber play, produced there with Hauptmann's *Hannele*.[38] It was ten times more effective than it would have been if the audience had had their knees in the orchestra and their backs against the wall of the pit. The Wagner Theatre in Bayreuth—a very big one—is the most "intimate" theatre in the world.[39] Besides, *The Admirable Bashville* is going to be a big production. The staging will be one of its great features. I am on my mettle this time, because comparisons will be unavoidable. Mr Tree has left everything at my disposal. All the treasures of his wardrobe, his scene dock, his property-room, all his cunning machines for simulating the warblings of the forest and the howling of the storm, all his resources in music and limelight, are under my hand to be lavished recklessly on *The Admirable Bashville*. And they will be. The whole staff of the theatre," continued Mr Shaw, with rising enthusiasm, "are unanimous in declaring that they have never seen a production even remotely resembling this one. And I think the public will say the same."

GORGEOUS SETTING AND LIMELIGHT

"Then you are going to rely at last on a gorgeous setting and plenty of limelight instead of on good acting?"

"Of course I am. But we shall have good acting, all the same. It will be, however, for the satisfaction of our own artistic instincts—for the pure love of acting. We shan't get any credit for it. Look at my cast! I could give a first-rate Shakespearean revival with it. Yet the critics will yawn in its face, most likely. Years ago, when Irving revived *Cymbeline*, one of the most beautiful things in it was the recital of the dirge by Ben Webster and Gordon Craig.[40] The reward they got was to have the last verse cut out, so as to get the tiresome business of an exquisite delivery of one of the loveliest passages in English literature made as short as possible. Well, Gordon Craig has taken himself and his touching voice and his hereditary genius for acting behind the scenes—his wonderful mother[41] ought to bring him back by the scruff of his neck—or I would have him in my cast. As it is, I can only borrow his curtains, since nobody else knows what curtains ought to be. Webster, on the other hand, is still available, fortunately. He created the part of Cashel Byron in the original production of the piece at the late Imperial Theatre,[42] and did just as fine things with the verse as he did in *Cymbeline*. But nobody seemed to care particularly. Nobody will care now either, I suppose. He and James Hearn and Henry Ainley will deliver my verse as finely as verse has ever been delivered in my time—a feat that requires precious gifts of voice and accomplishments not to be gained without long and hard work. Marie Löhr and Rosina Filippi will have to do technically just what they would have to do as Desdemona and Emilia. But, bless you, they will get no credit for it; all that will be noticed is their good looks and the funny part of the business, which a baby could act and an idiot write. Good casts are the only luxuries I indulge myself with. As you know, I am a man of simple tastes and unpretentious habits. The best of everything is good enough for me."

THE CAST

"The cast is very largely the original cast, is it not?"

"Oh, no. Mr Webster and Mr Hearn are still Cashel and Cetewayo; Mr Quartermaine, who made a hit as Lucian Webber, will play him again. But Mr Ainley takes the title-part, created by Mr Farren Soutar. Miss Marie Löhr succeeds Miss Henrietta Watson, Miss Filippi succeeds Miss Fanny Brough, Mr Lennox Pawle succeeds the late William Wyes, Mr Sass succeeds Mr Pilling, and Mr Halliwell Hobbes succeeds Mr Aubrey Smith.[43] You will see by both sets of names that it was not easy to live up to the old standard; but we have done it, I think, though we could not better it."

"We all know that you have a high opinion of your play, Mr Shaw. You describe it in the programme as a masterpiece."

Mr Shaw held me with a glittering eye. "What do you understand by a masterpiece?"

"A work of consummate excellence, of course."

"Not a bit of it. A masterpiece is a bit of work done by a craftsman, when he becomes a master after completing his apprenticeship, to show his technical skill. It is usually some quite useless contraption. I had to write *The Admirable Bashville* to protect my property in my own novel, *Cashel Byron's Profession*, from threatened piracy, and I took the opportunity to produce a masterpiece to show that I had the Shakespearean technique at my fingers' ends if I chose to use it. Also, I wanted to give a practical proof of what I had so often alleged—that it is the easiest technique in the world. But the acting of it requires a very difficult technique, so that really there will be much more mastery shown by the actors than by the author. I may say that I am childishly fond of blank verse, and that my idea of happiness in a regenerated world is to write Elizabethan plays, and rehearse them every day. What has saved England from Elizabethanism on the stage is that, though any duffer can write Elizabethan plays, very few actors can act them tolerably. And so the duffers have been left unacted."

"You hold to it that Shakespeare was a mere twaddler?"

"You cannot reasonably ask me to hold to what I never said. But I do say that in comparison with such prose rhetoric as Hamlet's "What a piece of work is man," and the finest parts of the authorised translation of the Bible, such blank verse rigmaroles as "The Seven Ages of Man" deserve to be called doggerel. I could have written the hell scene in *Man and Superman*, or the parts of the Priest Keegan in *John Bull's Other Island* and Undershaft in *Major Barbara*, much more easily in blank verse than in prose, at once rhetorical, poetic, and apparently colloquial. You may thank your stars that I resisted the temptation to be lazy."

BASHVILLE IRRESISTIBLY RIDICULOUS

"You reserve blank verse for burlesque, then?"

"No, *Bashville* is not a burlesque. It is certainly irresistibly ridiculous, but that effect is produced by simply applying the Elizabethan form strictly to a modern familiar situation. The euphemism and extravagance of the lines do not go a step beyond the ordinary practice of Shakespeare. I have occasionally patched in actual Shakesperean lines to show that the patches are never noticeable; they fit imperceptibly into my own stuff. A more convincing proof is that Mr Webster, at the first performance, brought the house down in serious applause more than once in the passages where the Elizabethan style happened to fit the sentiments expressed."

"I presume we shall have other revivals of your plays at the Afternoon Theatre?"

"Don't presume anything of the kind. One of the reproaches levelled at the Vedrenne and Barker experiment at the Court Theatre was that it proved nothing except that there was a select public for my plays. But the Afternoon Theatre has had an instantaneous success with plays by Hauptmann and Mack, without a thought of me. Do not forget that *The Admirable Bashville* is only a curtain raiser for George Paston's play, *Tilda's New Hat*,[44] which is to be the "pièce de résistance" next Tuesday. What makes *Bashville* important is the cast, and the cast alone. The absence of plays by me will, I hope, be a feature of the Afternoon Theatre season. Good work can be got from younger men without my mannerisms, and my fatal power of hypnotizing the Press into irritated imbecility. I have other things to do—at the Portsmouth Labour Conference,[45] for instance, so I must ask you to excuse me. Good morning."

And with that hasty hand-shake Mr Shaw hurriedly dashed away, as though suddenly awakened to the fact that the next train to Portsmouth started in ten minutes, and the fate of nations hung upon his catching it.

And then came Press Cuttings, *along with controversy. Written for the London Society for Women's Suffrage, the play is overtly political, two central characters, Prime Minister Balsquith and General Mitchener, being a thinly disguised amalgam of four prominent politicians (Arthur Balfour, Herbert Asquith, Alfred Milner, and Herbert Kitchener). The Lord Chamberlain denied the play a licence, causing the cancellation of a scheduled performance for 6 July 1909 at the Royal Court. Shaw wrote in protest to* The Times *on 26 June 1909 (and again on 30 June) and drafted an interview for the* Observer *for 27 June (all reprinted in Shaw,* Collected Plays *3:884-92). During the controversy Watson was in touch with Shaw, seeking information to compete with rival newspapers. Shaw responded with a letter on 30 June 1909.*

5. [TLS]

10 Adelphi Terrace
London W.C.

30 June 1909

Dear Malcolm Watson,

My relations with the monarchy grow daily more unfortunate. As you know, one of the three heroines of *Press Cuttings* was to have been played by Miss Gertrude Kingston,[46] who has already rehearsed the part to an extraordinary pitch of perfection. And now comes the King and deliberately commands a performance of Mrs Cornwallis West's play on the same afternoon. Miss Kingston is indispensable to Mrs Cornwallis West's play. One public man should not interfere with another in this manner. If the royal power is to be used to break up my casts, then the title of my next play will be *Cromwell*.

I have no further personal news concerning the Lord Chamberlain's department and *Press Cuttings*. The department does not easily change its mind, because such an operation is rather difficult without a mind to change. It has, however, shewn its usual aptitude for making mischief in unexpected quarters. The German press has got hold of the fact that my forbidden play makes hay of the anti-German war scare. It immediately scents anti-German opinions in St. James's Palace.[47] I am accordingly invited to ventilate my grievance in the German papers. In vain do I protest that to suspect the Lord Chamberlain's department of political ideas, or of any ideas whatsoever, is to shew the grossest ignorance of our censorship. Very naturally such protests will not wash in Germany after the sensation caused by the performance of *An Englishman's Home*—which, let me tell you, by the way, is no mere catchpenny topical piece, but a really good play by a writer who evidently has genuine dramatic talent. However, when that play, which represents a German invasion in a most transparent of disguises, is not only licensed by the Lord Chamberlain, but is made the subject of a special announcement that he will not permit Mr Pelissier[48] or anybody to burlesque it; and when, immediately after this, there comes the news that a play which disparages the war scare has been refused a license on a pretext which will not bear a moment's examination, what do you expect the German press to think? What should we think if the same thing happened in Germany? If we had no censorship, nobody in the world would dream of attaching any sort of political significance to either *An Englishman's Home* or my own trumpery little sketch. As it is, I expect the King will have to pay another visit to Berlin and bring the Lord Chamberlain and Mr Redford[49] with him in order to give the German nation an ocular demonstration of how entirely guiltless both gentlemen are of the large-minded European designs attributed to them.

Yours ever
G. Bernard Shaw

Watson ignored the issues concerning An Englishman's Home, *but wrote about* Press Cuttings *in the* Telegraph *on 1 July 1909, announcing the Court performances for the evenings of 9 and 12 July, "when, however, no money will be taken at the doors, admission being by tickets only purchased beforehand. Thus does Mr Shaw elude the vigilance of the Licenser" (see Shaw's corrections to Watson's announcement in the following letter). Watson also defended the censorship of* Press Cuttings *on the grounds that William Gilbert's and Gilbert A. À Beckett's satire* The Happy Land *was "an excellent precedent . . . for ruling that the living presentment of well-known political personages on the stage should be forbidden." That didn't go down well with Shaw, who wrote immediately to Watson to put him right.*

6. [TLS]

10 Adelphi Terrace, W.C.

1 July 1909

Dear Malcolm Watson,

You have not yet got the hang of this censorship business. *The Happy Land* was not stopped by the Lord Chamberlain. It was licensed and played both in London and all over the country. What the Lord Chamberlain did was to put a stop to the three principal actors making up like Gladstone, Lowe and Ayrton. And even this he could only do in London. I saw the piece myself in Dublin with the make-up all complete.[50] Exactly the same thing happened later on in a piece called, I think, *Have You Seen The Shah?*[51] In that piece the Shah appeared with his celebrated necklace of diamonds replaced by a necklace of pawntickets, and danced jigs and did all kinds of monstrously undignified things. Again the Lord Chamberlain prevented the actor from making up like the Shah; and again prohibition had no effect outside London. I saw the part played by Royce in Dublin; and he was much more like the Shah than the Shah was himself. Consequently the piece you mention is not only not a precedent for the censoring of *Press Cuttings*, but a precedent for the licensing of it. Even on the point of make-up, an actor can make up like Balfour or make up like Asquith; but if you can tell us how to make up like Balsquith, we shall be much obliged to you.

The precedent which is staring everybody in the face is Barrie's *Josephine*,[52] in which Chamberlain was caricatured as Josephine, and Balfour as Arthur. Now it is pretty clear that a Censor who passes Arthur and Josephine and objects to Mitchener and Balsquith has some other reason in the background.

I explained all this in an interview in last Sunday's *Observer* except the point about *The Happy Land*, which had not then been trotted out.[53]

Your announcements are in a hideous mess. The two performances are not to be in the evening but in the afternoon. If the license is withheld, tickets will not be sold at all. What will happen is that a new body called The Civic and Dramatic Guild will invite members of the Women's Suffrage Society and others to two At Homes at the Court Theatre; and Forbes Robertson will recite *The Ancient Mariner* to the invited guests. *Press Cuttings* will also be run through for their amusement. People who desire invitations should address themselves to any member of the Society or to the Secretary at 58 Victoria Street.

Yours ever,
G. Bernard Shaw

The private performance of Press Cuttings *went ahead at the Court on 9 July 1909 (repeated on 12 July), not only with the Forbes Roberston reading, but also a performance of a one-act play by Sidonie Culton called* The Fair Arabian, *which "showed how an Arab woman outwitted a jealous husband and an amorous tourist" (*The Times, *10 July 1909). The* Telegraph *reviewed* Press Cuttings *on 10 July: "It is a humorous and somewhat incoherent piece of badinage, in which the author does his best to laugh at political leaders, heads of the Army, the peerage, the Constitution, and the Anti-Suffragists." After Shaw changed the name of Mitchener to Bones and Balsquith to Johnson,* Press Cuttings *was licensed for performance, first at the Gaiety Theatre in Manchester on 27 September 1909 and then at the Kingsway in London on 21 June 1910, under the auspices of the Women's Suffrage Society, "of whose cause Mr Shaw is the declared champion." (See Nicholson 43-44.)*

Misalliance *was the next Shaw play to attract Watson's attention. It premièred at the Duke of York's Theatre on 23 February 1910 in American theatre manager Charles Frohman's (1860-1915) repertory season, which opened on 21 February 1910 with Galsworthy's* Justice. *Directed by Shaw himself,* Misalliance *mustered only eleven performances over a six-week period. Watson wrote to Shaw a few days before the opening. As usual, Shaw responded with a script, disguising it this time—sensitive to Frohman's authority—as "a casual conversation." Watson* published it in the Telegraph *on 18 February 1910*,⁵⁴ *adding the usual deceptive histrionics: ". . . it was only by a happy chance . . . that I succeeded yesterday in waylaying [Mr Shaw] and in extricating from him something regarding the piece."* The Telegraph *review of* Misalliance *is in the Appendix, p. 77.*

7. [ANS]

[February 1910]⁵⁵

[No salutation]

Sorry to be so late; but I am overwhelmed with work just now. Use it as a note of a casual conversation with you personally, not as a special communication from me to the D.T., as I have no right to make any without consulting Frohman.

G.B.S.

[HD]

Notes for an informal interview on *Misalliance*

The play is really a set of variations on themes from Mr Granville Barker's *Madras House*, Mr Charles McEvoy's *David Ballard*, and the daily papers, including the Selfridge advertisements, not to mention Zola's *Bonheur des Dames*.⁵⁶ Its chief feature will be its inordinate length. It is well to make audiences suffer: people remember their calamities more vividly than their pleasures: hence my reputation and the comparative obscurity of those mistaken playwrights who seek only to please. Most of the characters are what is called undramatic: that is, they have a reasonable control of their passions and attach a considerable value to money. I do not see why there should be any curiosity concerning my play: I have not been born again since I wrote all the other ones. The goods will be of the quality for which the firm is famous; and the press will say the usual things about them. Everybody knows how Mr Charles Frohman presents plays at the Duke of York's Theatre; and if everybody does not know how I write them, it is not for lack of opportunity. The title *Misalliance* means exactly what it always means. No: it is not a French word: it is a naturalized English one. The play, like all my plays, and like all the best modern English plays, is not based on the conventions of the French theatre or the Italian opera, but on the familiar realities of English life. No doubt a certain number of foolish people will get into a distorted unnatural, and unnecessarily clever attitude to receive it, and then revenge their self-inflicted discomfort on me by accusing me of their own folly. I'm sorry for them; but I can't help them. Unsophisticated people who don't make trouble for themselves will like it as they generally like my plays, and will wonder what on earth the other people are complaining about. Any difficulty with the Lord Chamberlain? No: after a prolonged scrutiny he passed it like a lamb. I can't imagine what he was thinking about. Probably he didn't understand it. Or perhaps the announcement of the 275th performance of *Mrs Warren's Profession* in Berlin[57] has broken his once buoyant spirit.

Frohman announced plans for further repertory seasons in Watson's weekly column in the Telegraph *on 9 June 1910, but nothing came of them.*[58] *Frohman continued to produce plays in London, but not in a repertory system. In the same column Watson fuelled rumours of a Shaw-Barker management "as managers and controllers of a West-end theatre of their own." He wrote to Shaw about this, hoping, it seems, for something he could use in his weekly column. But Shaw's response—owing to lack of time, it seems—was uninformative (while not entirely dismissive of the notion of a Shaw-Barker management). Watson must also have asked Shaw about plans for a production of* The Chocolate Soldier, *the Oscar Straus musical adaptation of* Arms and the Man *(which had already been produced in Vienna and New York). Watson subsequently announced the British première (The Lyric Theatre, 10 September 1910) in the* Telegraph *on 18 August 1910, adding that "Mr Shaw ... has only acquiesced in the presentation of the opera on the condition that none of the dialogue in* Arms and the Man *be used."* The Chocolate Soldier *ran at the Lyric for 500 performances—with not a penny in royalties for Shaw.*

8. [ALS]

Ayot St. Lawrence, Welwyn, Herts.

15 June 1910

[No salutation]

Your letter reaches me too late to be of any use this week.
There is nothing settled; but it is now clear that nothing but a Barker-Shaw theatre can keep our plays on the stage in London. Probably someone will start one, because there is a living in it. All the ordinary managers are not out for livings, but for fortunes.
    They are quite welcome to play their Chocolate Soldier provided they don't pretend that it's my *Chocolate Soldier*, and don't crib my dialogue. I have not

refused anything, and have no reason to suppose that the piece cannot be played here as easily as in Vienna or New York.

G.B.S.

Apart from two charity performances of The Dark Lady of the Sonnets *in support of the Shakespeare Memorial National Theatre appeal at the Haymarket on 24 and 25 November 1910, no new work by Shaw was seen in London until* Fanny's First Play, *which opened at the Little Theatre on 19 April 1911. Lillah McCarthy*[59] *had taken over the lease of the theatre from Gertrude Kingston for a season in 1911 while Kingston was resting on doctor's orders (as Kingston explained in a letter to* The Times *on 14 March 1911). Rumours had been circulating in the press about McCarthy's plans for the Little, plans that perhaps included a new play by Shaw. Watson looked to Shaw for information—to no avail on this occasion.*

9. [ALS]

Ayot St. Lawrence, Welwyn, Herts.

22 March 1911

[No salutation]

I saw a sporting statement in *The Referee* as to Miss McCarthy's intentions.[60] All I can say is that I have no doubt she will produce a play by me if she can get it. She will also produce a play by Barrie if she can get it. Perhaps she has got it. Ask Barrie.[61]

G.B.S.

Shaw, for reasons that eventually became apparent, was keeping mum about McCarthy's plans. "There is," Watson reported to his Telegraph *readers on 6 April 1911, "a distinct air of mystery" about what McCarthy was up to. "For the time being the author has sternly forbidden any mention of either his own name or that of the piece. 'All I can say,' Miss McCarthy declared yesterday, 'is that he is a well-known playwright, and that his name begins with a B.'" That set the critical tongues a-wagging. Watson came up with (James) Barrie, (Rudolf) Besier, (Max) Beerbohm, (Charles) Brookfield, or "if written with a hyphen, Bernard-Shaw." "Why secrecy is to be maintained on the subject Miss McCarthy frankly admits she does not know." She did know, of course. It was Shaw's deliberate strategy,* abetted by McCarthy, to conceal his authorship in order to give the new play—on a controversial subject—a fair hearing.

Shaw was also concealing his authorship to heighten the fun he planned in lampooning three London theatre critics: A.B. Walkley of The Times (Trotter), E.A. Baughan of the Daily News (Vaughan), and Gilbert Cannan of The Star (Gunn). A fourth critic, Flawner Bannal, was a composite of all who offered the banal criticism to which Shaw had become accustomed. Notably absent from the list was a Daily Telegraph critic, which perhaps the paper took as a compliment—or maybe took offence at being excluded. Whatever the reason, for once the Telegraph chose not to review any new Shaw play, a play that turned out to have the longest run ever of a Shaw play: 623 performances (transferring from the Little to the Kingsway Theatre on 30 December 1911).

During the run of Fanny's First Play Watson wrote a surprisingly personal letter to Shaw about taxation matters, and received an informed and constructive reply. At the time that Watson contacted him, Shaw was taking a particular and very public interest in tax matters as someone directly affected by the new Supertax on high income earners implemented by Chancellor of the Exchequer David Lloyd George in his 1909 "People's Budget." (See Shaw's letters on tax issues in The Times in Ford 116-21.) The issue that exercised both Shaw and Watson was the lack of a legal requirement for women high earners (such as Shaw's wife) to declare their earnings from property holdings—and pay tax accordingly—separately from their husbands. The deficiency was remedied by a 1911 Revenue Bill ("the Bernard Shaw Relief Bill").

10. [ALS]

10 Adelphi Terrace, W.C.

20 October 1911

Dear Malcolm Watson,

My difficulty, which ended in the passing of the Bernard Shaw Relief Bill, was not over Income Tax but Supertax. Under the Income Tax Acts a wife can be assessed separately from her husband if she is carrying on a business, but not if her income is derived from property. She can now be assessed separately for property in the case of Supertax by the new Act. I presume it applies also to Income Tax; but I am not quite sure.

However, your case is clearly one in which your wife carries on a business. If you state that you do not know what your wife's earnings are; that she will not disclose them to you on principle; and that you have no means of making her do so, I do not see how they can assess you unless the new Act has omitted Income Tax. If you are claiming an abatement on the ground that your income is less than £700 a year, then that complicates the matter. But supposing you return your income as £500, and state that you claim no abatement, as your wife's income, though you do not know its exact amount, certainly brings the joint income above the £700 limit, then I think they would be bound to extract a separate return from your wife if she has not already made one. I believe the new Act gives them power to do this. She MUST make the return or languish in Holloway[62] for contempt of court.

You see, their only way of getting at a recalcitrant wife hitherto has been to put a fancy assessment on the wretched husband, and thereby force him to prove to them that the assessment is excessive by shewing them his wife's accounts, leaving him to induce her to disclose them to him by blandishments or by beating her with the poker. This is what they are doing in your case. I should say everything depends on whether your wife will make a return of her earnings under Schedule D. If they get that, and get your own statement, they must assess you separately, though they may add the two together for the purpose of deciding whether you are entitled to an abatement or not. The overwhelming argument for this is that if your wife were earning £6000 a year as an actress and chose to leave you and give you either nothing at all or £1 a week, she might, unless they forced her to pay under the new Act, evade income tax altogether by simply referring them to her husband. They would then apply to you for £415 Income Tax and Supertax. Obviously they would not get it. Pelt them with this reductio ad absurdum.

I am assuming that their guess at your wife's earnings as equal to your own is an excessive one. I need hardly remind you that if she has earned more than you, and you live happily together in a state of communism as to your incomes, you will save money by accepting their estimate without protest. But in that case you will be defrauding the Revenue, which I trust is repugnant to your nature as a citizen.

Yours ever,
G. Bernard Shaw

P.S. You understand that my wife did not refuse to make a return. What she objected to was being treated as a mere appendage of her husband.

Given Shaw's reputation as a cerebral, albeit witty, playwright—a reputation that Watson helped create and confirm—it is not surprising that, like other critics, Watson was somewhat bemused in late 1911 by the presence of a Shaw play on the bill of a variety theatre, competing for the attention of a less-than-cerebral audience with, for example, Arabian dancers, acrobats, light musical interludes, bioscopes, animal acts, and impersonators. Thus when it became known that How He Lied to Her Husband,[63] directed by Shaw himself, was scheduled for production at the Palace Theatre in London, Watson was eager to get Shaw's explanation. Shaw was forthcoming, but again controlled the interview by drafting it himself. Watson wanted to talk about the apparent incompatibility of a Shaw play and variety theatre; Shaw's priority was to talk about his ongoing opposition to theatre censorship. He had attended the annual dinner of the Actors' Association on 3 December (the day before he wrote the interview) at which Herbert Beerbohm Tree, a supporter of theatre censorship, had spoken benignly (as reported in The Times, 4 December 1911) about the recently appointed (The Times, 27 November 1911) new Joint Examiner of Plays (with G.A. Redford), Charles Brookfield (1857-1913). Shaw was particularly agitated by the appointment of a practising playwright whose theatrical (and political) values were diametrically opposed to his own.

There is no letter attached to the part-typescript, part-holograph document that Shaw prepared for Watson, but Watson has written an initialled (undated) note in the margin of the first page, "This is G.B. Shaw's reply to my request that he would give me an interview." Watson published the interview in the Telegraph on 5 December 1911, which also included a brief review of How He Lied to Her Husband in the same issue (see Appendix, p. 81).

Watson introduced the published version of the interview with the statement that "It was a private matter . . . that took me to see Mr Bernard Shaw," but "the chance was too good to be lost . . . to obtain from the latest dramatist-recruit to the variety stage some indication of his views regarding the music-hall." This could well be another of Watson's many pretences that a meeting and interview with Shaw had actually taken place. On this occasion, however, it is just possible that Watson was actually telling the truth, perhaps having arranged to visit Shaw to follow up on the personal tax matters he had raised a few weeks earlier (see Shaw's letter, above, 20 October 1911). Even so, there is no doubt that Shaw's "views regarding music-hall" were put in writing as a script for Watson to reproduce in the Telegraph on 5 December.

11. [TD and HD]

[December 1911]

"I am sorry to have kept you waiting," said Mr Shaw; "but I have just been at a forbidden performance."

"Mrs Warren's Profession?"

"Oh no. Something much worse. Played before an audience largely consisting of bishops too. Forbidden incidents. Forbidden language. Forbidden characters. A gross defiance of censorship."

"But what can you possibly mean, Mr Shaw? What characters? What language? What incidents?"

"You'll hardly believe. Joseph, for instance."

"Mr Chamberlain?"

"Great Heavens, no: this was a Christmas play; and one does not associate Mr Chamberlain particularly with Christmas: at least I don't. No: I mean <u>the</u> Joseph. Joseph and Mary, and the three Kings, and the shepherds abiding in the field, and Simeon, and Lazarus and all the Bible people. You ask what incidents. What do you think of the Annunciation as an incident? What do you think of the Nativity as an incident? There was only one character in the whole play that the Censor would have passed; and he has passed her so often under various names that he could hardly refuse her now under her best known one."

"Mary Magdalen?"

"Precisely. I see you know the practice of the Lord Chamberlain's office thoroughly. This outrage on him is being perpetrated at the Imperial Institute,[64] the lay Cathedral of the empire. The performance is extraordinarily impressive and touching; and the stage pictures are among the most beautiful I have seen. Note also the work of a woman—Mrs P.D.[65] And the acting is something to rejoice in. To me as an author there is a special delight in seeing artists who have worked with me, and whose rarest qualities so seldom find an opportunity in such plays as we are allowed to write for them, getting, if only for a moment, some dignified and beautiful work to do. It makes me proud of my association with them and of the English theatre. But of course this play is not licensed. It is not like *Dear Old Charley* [sic].[66] As a Christian Morality it is not entitled to the privileges of a Palais Royal farce; and Mrs Percy Dearmer ranks officially as an improper person, who can never aspire to Mr Brookfield's sheaf of two guinea certificates of propriety from the King's household."[67]

"On the subject of Mr Brookfield's appointment, Mr Shaw"—

"I should prefer to keep off it. Nothing that I can say can add to the eloquence with which the situation speaks for itself. However, there is a suggestion which I venture to make publicly to Mr Brookfield, whom I have not the pleasure of knowing privately. At present he is a practising dramatist. His plays are on the stage and in the market in competition with those of his fellow-playwrights. Thus he has a direct pecuniary interest in suppressing rival plays, especially plays which are likely to lead the public taste away from the sort of work with which his name is connected. Clearly, when he enters on his functions as official dictator of British morality he must definitely retire from business as a playwright and withdraw all his plays from commercial representation.[68] Otherwise a scandal would arise very much as if a judge trying patent cases was himself a practising commercial inventor with half a dozen patents in his own pocket. I do not doubt that Mr Brookfield will do the correct thing; but it would be wise to give the public an explicit assurance to that effect, as, if Mr Brookfield's action were not made known, the effect would be as bad as if he were to retain his interests."

"No doubt he will take the hint. But what I have called about, Mr Shaw, is your first appearance next as a variety theatre author at the Palace. That has surprised a good many people."

"A good many people are always surprised at any piece of commonsense on my part, especially if I have been advocating it strongly for the last twenty years. Why on earth should I not allow my plays to be performed at a variety theatre?"

"But the association with performing dogs—"

"My good sir, no sensible west end variety theatre ever lets a performing dog within a mile of its stage door. It acts like a good watch dog—keeps the public out. But when dogs are not made to do melancholy and unnatural things that no happy dog would attempt, I like their company, and, if necessary, their co-operation. Sir Herbert Tree played with a dog in *Richard II*, and a very nice dog it was.[69] I did not object to write a play for Sir Herbert, though the censor would not allow him to play it because it had religious tendencies.[70] The real difficulty about variety theatres is that the standard of training, accomplishment, and professional skill is so high, and the standard of stage effect so swift, intense & miraculous, that it is very much harder to come up to concert pitch there than in an ordinary theatre. Dancers, acrobats, jugglers and strong men are terrible people to compete with. They are trained to the last inch, skilled to the point of doing with ease and certainty things that are impossible to their audiences—that seem superhuman. This gives them amazing distinction. It may not occur to you to call them distinguished; but if you are rash enough, immediately after one of their performances, to send an undistinguished actor or actress on the stage—somebody who would pass muster quite well in an ordinary theatre—the audience misses that distinction, at once; and the actor looks hopelessly unskilled and unattractive. You will observe that though my play at the Palace is a trifle, the artists who are working with me there, Miss Halstan, Mr Harcourt Williams and Mr Dawson Milward, have always played leading parts in my longer and more serious plays.[71] I dare not venture at The Palace, even for a half an hour, with anything less than the strongest talent I can get. Nothing less could hold its own there. Why then should I pretend—or should you pretend for me—that I am condescending in any way in going to a variety theatre? On the contrary, I regard Mr Butt's[72] invitation as a considerable compliment; and I only hope the results will justify him."

"Do you intend to write specially for the halls—I beg pardon, for the variety theatres?"

"Certainly I do. I have proved that I cannot[73] write longer plays than anyone else: now I am going to prove that I can write shorter ones. Besides, one of my finest heroines is an acrobat. You remember what a charming acrobat Miss Lena Ashwell was in *Misalliance*?[74] Well, why should not some wonderful acrobat—say Lina Pantzer[75]—make a charming heroine for me some day? All actors and actresses should graduate as dancers, acrobats, variety artists. The other day I was talking to some very fortunate and gifted actresses. I asked them had they ever wanted to be actresses. They said no. I asked hadn't they longed to be acrobats. They said yes with a rush. So had I. I love trained people. I hate sloppy people. Well, the only sloppy people you ever see in a variety theatre are the people who are padded into shapelessness for the purpose of being knocked down. No: depend on it, the variety theatres will smarten us all up, authors as well as actors. The notion that Mr Barrie, Mr Sutro, Mr Henry Arthur Jones, the late Sir William Gilbert[76] and all the other authors who, like myself, have taken their appearance on the variety stage as a matter of course, knew perfectly well what they were about. It is curious, after their action, that my own should give rise to any comment. But I seem to have the gift of surprising people extremely whenever I do what everybody else does. I wish I hadn't. Good afternoon."

There is a gap in the Shaw-Watson narrative after the performance of How He Lied to Her Husband *at the Palace, though the* Telegraph, *of course, sustained its professional attention to Shaw. (See, for example, the lukewarm review of* Androcles and the Lion *on 2 September 1913, Appendix, p. 81.)*

But early in 1914 curiosity began to build around reports of a new Shaw play called Pygmalion. *As speculation in the press about* Pygmalion *grew in the weeks preceding its London opening at His Majesty's Theatre on 11 April 1914—with great emphasis on rumours (aided and abetted by Shaw) that Mrs Patrick Campbell's Eliza would utter a scandalous word—Shaw began to worry that the play would be a victim of its own success even before it opened. Would the reaction of an excited and excitable audience prevent* Pygmalion *from being taken seriously? Thus it was that Shaw sought Watson's help in trying to exercise some influence over audience behaviour for the much-anticipated* Pygmalion *opening. The article that appeared in the* Telegraph *on 8 April 1914, again parading as a conversation with Shaw, was in fact another self-drafted interview.*[77]

MR BERNARD SHAW ON FIRST NIGHTERS

Ninety-nine playwrights out of a hundred will cheerfully—or perhaps it is more correct to say dismally—confess that they look forward to the first stage performance of a piece with something like a feeling of absolute dread.

Mr Bernard Shaw is not one of them, as you will quickly gather if, as I did yesterday, you ask him how he feels regarding next Saturday evening at His Majesty's Theatre.

"No," he emphatically said, "I am not at all anxious as to the representation of *Pygmalion* on Saturday. With such a cast, and after the pains that have been taken with the preparation—the production, as people call it—there can be no ground for the smallest anxiety on that score.[78] The question is, will the first night audience give the play a chance? Will the hygenic gentlemen, who have been told by their doctors that there is nothing so good for the lungs as a hearty five minutes' guffaw, be there? Will the kindly people who think it encourages the poor, dear actors to be interrupted at every tenth word by shouts of appreciation all be laid up with influenza, as I most fervently hope they may? Will the faithful pilgrims who come long distances and sit on the steps of the theatre all day to secure a front seat, and devote their whole souls to giving receptions to their idols at the most disconcerting moments, will they be there?

PUBLIC AND PLAYWRIGHTS

If so, you may put the idea of an artistic performance out of your head; the thing is impossible. The continuity of the play will be lost; all the transitions from one mood to another, which cost so much artistic study and work to perfect, will be obliterated; the performers, trying to concentrate themselves on a long and difficult task, will be distracted and forced to give up all attempt at fine work in despair; the spectators will be worried by their own noisy enjoyment; and, finally, they will lose their trains and go home half an hour late, cross and tired, and have words with one another, ending with, 'I will never go to the theatre with you again while I live.'

That is the sort of thing that happened at the first night of *Androcles and the Lion*,[79] which was such a horrible experience that the next first-night—that of the revival of *The Doctor's Dilemma*—was deliberately fixed so as to clash with that of *The Night Hawk*, which took all the regular first-nighters away.[80] The result was most successful. But there is nothing to clash with *Pygmalion*, and I suppose we shall have the usual well-intended, good-natured riot that is the disgrace of the English theatre. Why on earth don't people laugh internally, like old Weller in *Pickwick*?[81] I can't understand why the Playgoers' Club or the Club of First Nighters do not take up this question, and insist on the right of a play to be heard as attentively as a music drama by Wagner or Strauss."

"But do you seriously expect an audience to listen in dead silence, no matter how funny the lines are?"

LAUGHTER A BAD HABIT

"I do not see why they should not; loud laughter is merely a bad habit. But I am not myself a dead silent playgoer. At the first night of Sir James Barrie's *Adored One*,[82] a gentleman said to me, as I left the stalls, 'You object to anyone else laughing in the theatre, but you have been laughing yourself all through the play.' So I had been; but my laughter did not interrupt the performance, nor prevent my neighbours catching the next words of the play, nor interfere with the concentration of the actors on their parts.

Pygmalion, which is in five acts, will last until church time on Easter Sunday morning [Sunday 12 April] if the first-nighters refuse to contain their tears, cheers, and laughter until the ends of the acts. If that happens, I will in future cut out all the good things in my plays on the first night, and thus get the whole business finished in five minutes, of course giving complete printed copies to the critics. The whole question is one of good sense and good manners. It is only on first nights that people are obstreperous. They mean well. They think they are gratifying the performers and helping to make the evening a success. When they understand that they are really doing their utmost to ruin it, they will, I hope, oblige me by behaving in a reasonably continent way."

A SERIOUS PLAY

"But is *Pygmalion* irresistibly funny?"

"Not at all. There is nothing in it to force anyone to be uproarious or else burst. I can listen to it without yells of merriment; and I, as the author, ought to be more amused by it than anyone else. It is really a serious play, though the pill is sugared by the romance of a flower-girl changed into a lady by a gentleman whom she meets by accident on a wet night when they are both sheltering from the rain under the portico of St Paul's Church, in Covent-garden. But the tragedy comes in the fate of the flower girl's father, whose story is really a modern version of the old Don Juan play, *Il Dissoluto Punito*.[83] This man is an Immoralist, a lover of wine, women, and song, a flouter of respectability, one whose delight is to épater le bourgeois [*shock the bourgeoisie*].

In the old play he is cast into Hell by the statue of the man he has murdered. In my play a far more real and terrible fate overtakes him. No: it is not the fate of Oswald in Ibsen's *Ghosts*, nor of the young man in Brieux's *Les Avariés*.[84] Nothing like that at all. Something quite simple, quite respectable, quite presentable to the youngest schoolgirl. And yet a fearful retribution. The rest of the play is merely to call public attention to the importance of the study of phonetics, which has always been one of my favourite subjects.

Let me tell you one remarkable fact. The translation of the play into Swedish by Mr Hugo Vallentin[85] has been made extremely difficult by the fact, astounding to a Londoner, that in Stockholm all classes speak the same language. That is real civilization. Here a flower-girl speaks one language and a duchess another, though the difference is not so great as the duchess thinks, especially if she is a smart duchess. We shall never have a standard English until we have a National Theatre cooperating with a serious Academy of Letters. Not that either of them will do anything, but people will keep saying that they ought to do something; and that is how things finally get done."

"All this," I remarked, "sounds very serious. Retribution is rather dismal; and phonetics seem a trifle dry for dramatic fare."

"Not at all. To a properly trained mind there is nothing so succulent as the science of human speech."

"But you admit some romance. The flower-girl marries the gentlemen, of course?"

"Nothing of the kind. It would be illegal. She married somebody else last Monday."

A few days after the opening of Pygmalion, *Shaw wrote to Watson to thank him for his help in establishing what Shaw, somewhat optimistically, called "a new code of manners in the theatre." Watson reproduced Shaw's letter verbatim in the* Telegraph *on 18 April 1914, prefacing it thus: "Mr Bernard Shaw's prayers have at last prevailed. The public has responded, partially at any rate, to his appeal for silence during the performance of his plays, and he desires to place on record his grateful recognition of the fact. With this brief introduction it only remains for me to stand aside and allow Mr Shaw to express himself in his own characteristic fashion. This, then, is how he does so."*

12. [ALS]

Filey, Yorks,[86]

15 April 1914

Private or not, just as you like.

G.B.S.

Dear Malcolm Watson

I should like to acknowledge the handsome way in which the audience at the first night of *Pygmalion* responded to the appeal I made in your columns.[87] It was the beginning of a new code of manners in the theatre. There was an earnest attempt to secure an uninterrupted hearing for the play; and until the third act it was successful. And the quality of the applause at the end of the acts was delicious. I am a connoisseur in applause; and I can now certify that the people who appreciate a play finely enough to withhold their applause until the right moment are the people who give the best brand when that moment comes.

I am bound to add that when the audience did at last interrupt, it interrupted with a vengeance. But I did not quite mean them to resist Mrs Campbell's last speech in that act[88]—at least not for the first time. It was a hearty and delightful rebuke to the vulgar nonsense which had been written about it by some critics who ought to have known me better and known Mrs Campbell better than to fear that any passage we made ourselves responsible for would not justify itself in performance. Curiously enough, some of the writers who were the most stupid before the performance were the cleverest after it; so I forgive them, though I hope they won't do it again.

On the whole, not only do I not complain this time, but I am sincerely grateful for the general recognition that my appeal was a reasonable one and was made as much in the interest of the audience as in my own.

Yours ever
G. Bernard Shaw.

A very considerable gap occurs between the Pygmalion *correspondence and Shaw's next documented contact with Watson. During that time* Heartbreak House, Back to Methuselah, *and* Saint Joan *all had their London premières, and all were reviewed by the* Telegraph *(see Appendix, pp. 87, 89, 93).*

But, ironically, the next extant letter from Shaw to Watson concerns Shakespeare, not Shaw. On 6 March 1926 a fire destroyed the Shakespeare Memorial Theatre in Stratford, which had opened in 1879. The Telegraph *promptly set up a fund for a new theatre. Later that month, Watson, preparing a progress report for the paper, wrote to Shaw about the fund. Shaw replied:*

13. [ALS]

Ayot St. Lawrence, Welwyn, Herts.

23 March 1926

[No salutation]

I have already sent Flower 100 guineas, which is quite enough until we see what the appeal will bring in from America and elsewhere.

He tells me he has promised £1000. So make sure that your figure of £3000 is right before you publish it.

By the way I want £25,000 for the coming reconstruction of the Royal Academy of Dramatic Art when its lease expires. This is much more pressing than Stratford, which will actually carry on better without the horrid old theatre. But nobody will say a word for us.

G.B.S.

Watson drew on Shaw's response for a short piece on the fund in the Telegraph *on 26 March 1926, reporting that the fund "already exceeded" £5,000, which included Shaw's 100 guineas and a £1,000 commitment from Archibald D. Flower, Chair of the Board of Governors of the Memorial Theatre. A new theatre opened in 1932 on the same site as the original building. Watson did not mention Shaw's funding pitch for RADA, which opened a new building in 1927—helped by a £5,000 donation from Shaw (Gibbs, 263).*

Shaw's final letter to Watson is brief and cryptic.

14. [ALS]

Ayot St. Lawrence, Welwyn, Herts

18 December 1928

[No salutation]

I have no objection; but I think some other paper[89] has anticipated you: at least I seem to remember throwing away a press cutting about it.

G.B.S.

It is not immediately apparent what Shaw had "no objection" to, but the explanation comes in a short piece in the Telegraph *two days after Shaw's letter to Watson. In that piece (20 December 1928)—the piece to which Shaw had offered no objection— Watson reported that the* New York World *had recently given particulars of "a new play definitely stated to be the work of George Bernard Shaw." The play, it seems, was called* The Unknown Warrior. *Shaw, "in reply to inquiries" (from Watson), had told "a representative of* The Daily Telegraph" *(Watson) "I am not writing that play or anything like it." Shaw explained that on a visit to Geneva in September 1928 he had spoken about "'Le Tombeau sous l'Arc de Triomphe' and the suitability of the Unknown Warrior as the subject of a play," and had "described a plot which occurred to me that I did not use, nor have I any intention of using it."*[90]

By the end of 1928, Shaw, aged 72, still had lots of theatrical energy, with The Apple Cart *opening at the Malvern Festival, and other major plays to follow. Watson, however, was near the end of his career, and of his life. He retired from the* Daily Telegraph *at the end of July 1929, and just a few days later, in the early hours of 8 August 1929, after becoming ill at his London club, he died.*

NOTES TO THE LETTERS

1 Shaw and his wife, Charlotte, moved to this country address in November 1898. They lived there until August 1899, after which they made their home in a flat in Adelphi Terrace in central London.
2 Mrs Patrick Campbell ("P.C.") (1865-1940) played Cleopatra in the copyright performance of *Caesar and Cleopatra* in Newcastle on 15 March 1899, but not in the London (Savoy, 25 November 1907) or New York (New Amsterdam, 30 October 1906) premières. Johnston Forbes Roberston (1853-1937) was not in the Newcastle performance, but played Caesar in both London and New York, and co-directed (with Shaw) both productions—though Shaw was not present for the one in New York.
3 Forbes Roberston had played Macbeth at the Lyceum in 1898; the production ran for fifty-eight performances.
4 A woman of dubious morality (demi-reputable).
5 Shaw had sustained a serious foot infection in April 1898. It took several months (and an operation) to heal.
6 John Vedrenne (1867-1930) who, in collaboration with Harley Granville Barker (1877-1946), produced a repertory series at the Royal Court Theatre from 1904 to 1907. Eleven plays by Shaw established Shaw's reputation as a leading playwright. See Appendix, pp. 55–67, for a selection of *Daily Telegraph* reviews of the Court plays.
7 Unidentified, but presumably one of the event's organizers.
8 *Widowers' Houses*, *The Philanderer*, and *Mrs Warren's Profession* were published together as *Plays Unpleasant* in 1898. The most prominent "improper female" in them is Kitty Warren, brothel manager, in *Mrs Warren's Profession*.
9 Emma, Lady Hamilton (1765-1815) was best known as mistress to Lord Nelson, who defeated the French and Spanish navies at the Battle of Trafalgar (1805) but was killed in the battle. Catholic Mary Queen of Scots (1542-87) was imprisoned and subsequently executed by her Protestant cousin Elizabeth I, Queen of England (1533-1603).
10 Shaw presumably had in mind Arthur Wing Pinero's (1855-1934) *The Second Mrs Tanqueray* (St James's Theatre, 27 May 1893) and *The Notorious Mrs Ebbsmith*

(Garrick Theatre, 13 March 1895). Mrs Campbell played the title character in both productions.

11 An American actress (1872-1945) who moved to London in 1895. She was much admired by Shaw: "the best Celia I ever saw" (Dukore 716).
12 William Booth (1829-1912), founder of the Salvation Army.
13 Todger Fairmile in Act II, though he does not appear on stage.
14 Dan H. Laurence correctly identifies the article, as published, as a self-drafted interview (*Bibliography* C1494), but does not credit Watson's involvement. The interview is reprinted in Shaw, *Collected Plays* 3:186-89.
15 Shaw had been prompted, in part, to write *The Doctor's Dilemma* by an article William Archer (1856-1924) published in *The Tribune* (for which he was theatre critic) on 14 July 1906, "Death and Mr Bernard Shaw," in which Archer argued that Shaw was incapable of writing a convincing death scene. Shaw's response was the death of Dubedat in Act IV of *The Doctor's Dilemma*. On 3 September 1906 Shaw drafted a press release for Archer to publish in *The Tribune* announcing the play, and describing its death scene as "unlike any ever before represented." The full text of the press release is in Shaw, *Collected Plays* 3:437.
16 The interview is not included in Laurence's *Bibliography*.
17 Galsworthy's *The Silver Box* opened at the Royal Court on 25 September 1906 and ran for eight performances.
18 Stretton's novel *The Doctor's Dilemma* was published in 1872.
19 Jeremiah Joyce, *Scientific dialogues: intended for the instruction and entertainment of young people: in which the first principles of natural and experimental philosophy are fully explained* (1807). Shaw once denied (to Henry Arthur Jones) that he was "a doctrinaire . . . a sort of theatrical Joyce" (*Collected Letters* 1:462).
20 Laurence, *Bibliography* C1641, identifies the article as a self-drafted interview. It is reprinted in full in Shaw, *Collected Plays* 3:663-68, and, in part, in Evans 187-90. Watson is not credited in any of these instances.
21 He was also directing the play. The new play that Barker was working on was probably *The Madras House*, which opened at the Duke of York's Theatre on 9 March 1910.
22 *The Chinese Lantern* opened at the Haymarket on 16 June 1908 and ran for six performances. *Prunella* opened at the Royal Court on 23 December 1904 and ran for twenty-eight performances.
23 Manager of the Savoy Theatre.
24 On 4 June 1907. For the *Telegraph* review see Appendix, p. 66.
25 Charles Ricketts (1866-1931), illustrator, book designer, and set and costume designer for Shaw, Wilde, and other playwrights. He designed sets and costumes for the British première of *Saint Joan* (New Theatre, 26 March 1924); the *Telegraph* did not deem them worthy of comment (see the review, Appendix, p. 93).

26 British composer and conductor; dates unknown.
27 "The one thing that is certain is that it is not a play," said the *Telegraph* (below, p. 56).
28 The Tivoli and London Pavilion were variety halls; the Queen's Hall was a classical concert venue.
29 Shaw is referring to two long articles by Webb in *The Times* on 11 and 16 October 1906 in which Webb argued that what in his view was a disastrous decline in the birth rate in Great Britain was caused by economic circumstances that required government intervention.
30 Charles Gore (1853-1932), Bishop of Birmingham 1905-11, and Mandall Creighton (1843-1901), Bishop of London 1897-1901.
31 Identified by Laurence as a self-drafted interview (*Bibliography* C1644).
32 Identified by Laurence as a self-drafted interview (*Bibliography* C1666). Reprinted in Shaw, *Collected Plays* 2:479-87.
33 American financier and industrialist John Pierpont Morgan (1837-1913). The "picture gallery" that Shaw refers to is now the Morgan Library and Museum on Madison Avenue.
34 Arthur Balfour (1848-1930), British Prime Minister 1902-05; Sir Oliver Lodge (1851-1940), physicist and Principal of the University of Birmingham 1900-20; Albert Wilberforce (1841-1916), grandson of William Wilberforce, Anglican priest, and Archdeacon of Westminster 1900-16. Edward VII (1841-1910), eldest son of Queen Victoria, reigned from 1901 to 1910. At a performance of *John Bull's Other Island* at the Court Theatre on 11 March 1905, the King laughed so hard that he broke his chair.
35 Whelen (1867-1955), Fabian writer and lecturer, was one of the founders of the Stage Society in 1899, under whose auspices several of Shaw's plays were produced, including the banned *Mrs Warren's Profession* in 1902.
36 Arthur Wing Pinero's (1855-1934) *The Thunderbolt* opened at St James's Theatre on 9 May 1908 and ran for fifty-eight performances. James Barrie (1860-1937) had several West End commercial successes, including *Peter Pan*, which had enjoyed annual revivals since its première at the Duke of York's Theatre on 27 December 1904 (150 performances).
37 Shaw admired the plays of Strindberg (1849-1912). He was one of the Swedish writers Shaw had in mind when he established the Anglo-Swedish Literary Foundation (for translating Swedish works into English) with the prize money from his 1925 Nobel Prize for Literature.
38 Margaret Mack's (1874-1950) *Emily* and Gerhart Hauptmann's (1862-1946) *Hannele* opened on a double bill at His Majesty's Theatre on 8 December 1908 in the Afternoon Theatre series, and ran for six performances.
39 The Bayreuth Festspielhaus, which opened in 1876, has a seating capacity of around 2,000. Richard Wagner (1813-83) was among Shaw's favourite composers.

40 Henry Irving's (1838-1905) version of *Cymbeline* opened at the Lyceum Theatre on 22 September 1896. Shaw reviewed it in the *Saturday Review* on 26 September 1896. He described Ben Webster's (1864-1947) and Edward Gordon Craig's (1872-1966) performances as Guiderius and Arviragus, respectively, as "desperate failures," while acknowledging that they rendered the dirge ("Fear no more the heat o'th' sun," Act 4 Scene 2) "admirably"—or at least what Irving had left of it; he "maimed" it, said Shaw by cutting the third (antiphonal) verse. The full review is in Dukore 2:660-66.

41 Craig was the son of Ellen Terry (1847-1928) and E.W. Godwin (1833-86).

42 There was a private amateur performance of *The Admirable Bashville* at the Pharos Club in Covent Garden on 14 December 1902, but the first professional performance was by the Stage Society at the Imperial Theatre on 7 June 1903. The Imperial Theatre opened as part of the Royal Aquarium and Winter Garden in Westminster in 1876. Renamed the Imperial in 1879, it closed in 1908.

43 The full casts of the Imperial and His Majesty's productions of *The Admirable Bashville* are in Mander and Mitchenson 79.

44 George Paston was the pseudonym for Emily Morse Symonds (1860-1936). *Tilda's New Hat* is a one-act comedy that opened at the Court Theatre on 8 November 1908 for a single performance. After its revival at His Majesty's (thirty-nine performances), it opened at Wyndham's Theatre (with a transfer to the Prince of Wales) on 21 October 1910 for a total of ninety-eight performances.

45 The conference ran from 27 January to 4 February 1909. Shaw delivered speeches on 28 and 29 January (Gibbs 184).

46 Gertrude Kingston (1862-1937), having rehearsed for the role of Mrs Banger in *Press Cuttings*, appeared in a royal command performance of Mrs George Cornwallis-West's (Mrs Patrick Campbell) *His Borrowed Plumes* at the Globe Theatre on 9 July 1909.

47 A royal residence, close to Buckingham Palace, and the location of the office of the Lord Chamberlain.

48 *An Englishman's Home* is a play by "A Patriot" (Guy du Maurier [1865-1915]) that opened at Wyndham's Theatre on 27 January 1909 and ran for 163 performances. It reflected and reinforced fear of a German invasion in years leading up to World War I. The play was reviewed by Watson in the *Telegraph* on 28 January 1909. He recognized it as a militaristic tract, but recorded the audience's "outburst of enthusiasm" at the end. A subsequent (1909) burlesque of *An Englishman's Home* by H.G. Pélissier was denied a licence. See Nicholson 36-38, 66. (Du Maurier was killed in action in Flanders, Belgium.)

49 George Alexander Redford served as Examiner of Plays from March 1895 to January 1912 (Stephens 158). The Lord Chamberlain in 1909 was Charles Robert Spencer, Viscount Althorp (1857-1922).

50 *The Happy Land* opened at the Court on 3 March 1873, in a production that made the general political satire specific by the costuming and make-up of three politicians, linking them clearly to Prime Minister William Gladstone, Chancellor of the Exchequer Robert Lowe, and Commissioner of Public Works Acton Smee Ayrton. The play's licence was removed until the specific had reverted to the general. See Stephens 119-22.

51 Shaw is perhaps referring to a farce by K.E. Hall called *The Shah*, first performed in 1873 in Coatbridge, Scotland (Nicoll 399), but, presumably, subsequently in Dublin. Edward William Royce (1841-1926) was a star of pantomime and burlesque.

52 Barrie's revue opened at the Comedy Theatre on 5 April 1906 and ran for twenty-three performances. *The Times* (6 April 1906) commented that "it cannot but be noticed that Mr Barrie has been allowed to do what no one has been allowed to do for a very long time—bring the contemporary political situation straight on to the stage and make fun of Prime Ministers, parties, and programmes under a thin but exquisitely woven veil of allegory." Joseph Chamberlain (1836-1914) was a leading politician, prominent at the time of Barrie's revue for opposing free trade. For Balfour see note 34.

53 Shaw's self-drafted interview was published in *The Obsever* on 27 June 1909. It is reprinted in Shaw, *Collected Plays* 3:886-89.

54 Not included in Laurence's *Bibliography*.

55 Shaw's note is undated, but Watson's "interview" with Shaw appeared in the *Daily Telegraph* on 18 February 1910, based on a meeting Watson had "yesterday."

56 Granville Barker's *Madras House* opened at the Duke of York's Theatre on 9 March 1910 as part of Frohman's repertory season (ten performances); McEvoy's *David Ballard* was a Stage Society production at the Imperial Theatre on 9 June 1907 (two performances); Zola's novel *Au Bonheur des Dames* was published in 1883. All three works, like *Misalliance*, involve retail businesses. Selfridge's, then and now an upper-crust department store, had opened a new store on London's Oxford Street in March 1909, accompanied by heavy advertising in the press.

57 At the Hebbel Theatre; announced in *The Times* on 14 February 1910. *Mrs Warren's Profession*, having been denied a licence in 1898, was still banned from public performance in Great Britain—and would be until 1925. There were no censorship issues with *Misalliance*.

58 Shaw gave an "interview" with *The Observer* about the demise of Frohman's Repertory venture. See Shaw, *Collected Plays* 4:256-62.

59 Lillah McCarthy (1876-1960) featured prominently in several Shaw plays. She received several plaudits in *Daily Telegraph* reviews. (See Appendix, *passim*.)

60 Not traced.

61 McCarthy presented a revival of Barrie's *Twelve-Pound Look* at the Little Theatre on 3 October 1911. It ran for eighteen performances.

62 A women's prison in London, opened in 1852, closed in 2016. In *Fanny's First Play* Fanny does time in Holloway for assaulting a policeman.
63 First produced in New York on 26 September 1904; first produced in England at the Court Theatre 28 February 1905.
64 A London venue featuring *inter alia* music, lectures, and historical tableaux.
65 Mrs Percy Dearmer (1872-1915), novelist and playwright, was the first wife of Percy Dearmer (1867-1936), Christian socialist, cleric, and scholar.
66 *Dear Old Charlie*, a farce adapted by Charles Brookfield from *Célimare le bien-aimé* (1863) by Eugène Labiche and Alfred-Charlemagne Delacour, opened in Newcastle on 17 May 1906, and was first seen in London at the Vaudeville Theatre on 2 January 1908. See also below, note 68. Brookfield was appointed Joint Examiner of Plays in 1911.
67 As primarily a tableau of biblical scenes, the nativity performance at the Imperial Institute was not subject to the Lord Chamberlain's censorship (unlike a scripted farce at the Palais Royal, a London variety theatre). As the person responsible for the nativity performance, Mrs Dearmer did not, therefore, have to apply for a licence from the Lord Chamberlain (at a cost of two guineas).
68 Brookfield didn't do this. *Dear Old Charlie* was produced at the Prince of Wales Theatre on 20 February 1912. It had, however, been licensed before he was appointed Joint Examiner. Brookfield wrote no new plays after his appointment.
69 In a two-performance run of *Richard II* at His Majesty's Theatre, 27-28 April 1910, as part of a London Shakespeare Festival.
70 Shaw wrote *The Shewing-up of Blanco Posnet* in 1909 for the Afternoon Theatre series at Tree's His Majesty's Theatre, but the play was deemed blasphemous by the Lord Chamberlain and denied a licence for performance. See Nicholson 42-43 and Shaw, *Collected Plays* 3:800-812.
71 Margaret Halstan (1879-1967), Harcourt Williams (1880-1957), and Dawson Milward (1862-1926). Halstan created the role of Gloria Clandon in *You Never Can Tell*; Williams played Valentine in a subsequent production of *You Never Can Tell*, and was the original Count O'Dowda in *Fanny's First Play*; Milward was the original Lomax in *Major Barbara*.
72 Alfred Butt (1878-1962), Managing Director of the Palace Theatre.
73 Shaw obviously intended "can." It was corrected in the published text in the *Telegraph*.
74 Lena Ashwell (1872-1957) created the role of Lina Szczepanowska in *Misalliance*; she "gave charm to the Polish lady," said the *Telegraph* (below, p. 79).
75 A Music Hall performer who specialized in tightrope walking.
76 Alfred Sutro (1863-1933), W.S. Gilbert (1836-1911). For Barrie see note 36.
77 Laurence, *Bibliography* C1928, where it is identified as a self-drafted interview, but Watson is not credited. A fragment of this interview is printed in Shaw,

Collected Plays 4:799-800, transcribed from a shorthand script held in the British Library, Add MSS. 50560 f181.
78 Wishful thinking on Shaw's part. The rehearsal process was, in fact, fraught with difficulties, largely arising from personal and professional tensions among Shaw, Beerbohm Tree (Higgins), and Mrs Campbell (Eliza). See Shaw, *Pygmalion* xxi-xxii and sources cited there.
79 St James's Theatre, 1 September 1913. For the *Telegraph* review, see Appendix, p. 81.
80 A play by Lechmere Worrall (b. 1874/75) and Bernard Merivale (1882-1939) that opened at the Globe Theatre on 6 December 1913, the same night that a revival of *The Doctor's Dilemma* opened at St James's Theatre.
81 Sam Weller in Charles Dickens' *Pickwick Papers* (1837).
82 Duke of York's Theatre, 4 September 1913.
83 On which Mozart's *Don Giovanni* is based, the full title of which is *Il dissoluto punito; ossia, il Don Giovanni* (*The Libertine Punished; namely, Don Giovanni*).
84 Syphilis. The young man in *Les Avariés* (1901) is named Georges Dupont.
85 Published in Stockholm in 1914 (Laurence, *Bibliography* A124c).
86 A coastal town in Yorkshire, where Shaw was visiting Sidney and Beatrice Webb.
87 On 8 April 1914; see above, p. 38.
88 I.e., "Not bloody likely" (Act III).
89 Unidentified.
90 Watson's piece is listed in Laurence, *Bibliography* C2684, but is mis-dated 20 December 1927. See also Stanley Weintraub, "Bernard Shaw and 'The Unknown Warrior,'" *Times Literary Supplement,* 13 November 1981.

APPENDIX: Selected *Daily Telegraph* Reviews of Shaw Plays

You Never Can Tell
Strand Theatre, 2 May 1900
Daily Telegraph, 3 May 1900

London today knows a good deal more of Mr George Bernard Shaw and his paradoxical wit than it did when *Widowers' Houses* and *Arms and the Man* half amused and half irritated those who were inquisitive enough to follow a clever writer into fields then fresh to his footsteps. We know now that Mr Shaw as a dramatist is never to be taken quite seriously—that when he is apparently building up a scene which in a more orthodox playwright's hands might reach a strong and moving conclusion, he is almost invariably leading his audience on a false scent and preparing merely to scoff at some cherished convention of the theatre. To tell the truth, this device, brought to a fine point in *The Devil's Disciple*, has grown somewhat stale, and it is a relief in many ways to meet Mr Shaw on ground where he is not tempted to annoy his audience with a series of malicious dramatic feints, but indulges them, for the most part, with those whimsical extravagancies of character and conversation that become his pen so well. Such may be said at once by way of praise of *You Never Can Tell*, a piece reckoned by the author among his "pleasant" plays, and produced for a series of matinées at the Strand Theatre yesterday afternoon by Messrs Yorke Stephens and James Welch. The first two acts, without doubt, are infinitely more diverting than anything else that Mr Shaw has yet given to the stage; and it is mainly because the author has unwisely spun the thin thread of his plot—such as it is—into four long acts that the end, weaker in all respects than the beginning, grows wearisome. Where a play depends solely and entirely on its dialogue, even Mr Shaw's witty pen must eventually fail him, and it is safe to say that of pure situation, turned either to comic or tragic account, *You Never Can Tell* gives us no sign. The story of the play can be told in a few words. [*A plot summary follows.*]

This seems little enough in the telling, but there is no denying the excellence of the talk which Mr Shaw puts into his puppets' mouths. Much of it, no doubt, fairly touches the regions of extravaganza; but much, on the other hand, has humanity as well as humour to commend it. In every part something of the author's individuality appears, but there are certainly two characters which Mr Shaw has drawn with a degree of truth and restraint that his abounding desire to say a "good thing" at the expense of somebody or something does not always permit him to exercise. Fergus Crampton, a man in whom paternal feelings have had to fight a desperate battle with an obstinate nature and a villainous temper, is a strong and convincing figure; while equally good in a quieter way is Mrs Clandon, a woman whom "advanced views" have taken far, but whose softer maternal instincts peep out at every turn. These parts are played by Hermann Vexin and Miss Elsie Chester, and each in its way is admirably carried through. More complicated efforts are made by the dramatist in the cases of the young lovers. But those playgoers who remember Old Sartorius's daughter in *Widowers' Houses*, and the fibbing heroine of *Arms and the Man*, will recognise in Gloria Clandon a creature after Mr Shaw's own heart. Like her predecessors, Gloria is no immaculate, and the author insists upon her weaknesses with the air of one who again declines to cumber his play with an attractive young lady unless he is permitted to show that even the stage has no right to a spotless heroine. In the acting, such a part as Gloria Clandon must be one of many difficulties, and it is no discredit to Miss Mabel Terry Lewis that she obviously felt those difficulties yesterday. As time passes on she will probably find that immobility may be carried too far, and that a little more play of face and gesture will do good rather than harm. Valentine, whom we first meet in the midst of a dentist's forbidding paraphernalia, pairs well with Gloria. He is no nearer to the ideal here than was Mr Shaw's "chocolate cream soldier," and Mr Yorke Stephens, taking him at his proper value, makes the most of his share of Mr Shaw's pretty wit. Of the more extravagant sketches in *You Never Can Tell* the happiest are the two younger Clandons, Philip and Dolly. The precocious egotism of the boy and the unabashed inquisitiveness of the girl are equally outrageous, but so liberally has the author furnished this delightful pair with "lines" that snap like crackers that one cannot but accept them with thankfulness. Miss Audrey Ford and Mr W. Graham Browne have these pleasant opportunities, and make quite the best of them. A garrulous and confiding waiter, who pervades many scenes in the play, might easily be turned by an injudicious actor into a burlesque figure, especially when to this impossible attendant there enters his son, an eminent and equally impossible Q.C. Mr James Welch, however, does his chattering and liquour-serving with great discretion, and so almost persuades his audience that a seaside hotel might really bring forth so pronounced a curiosity. Mr George Raiemond, too, plays well as a well-meaning but crushed solicitor.

But, above any individual effort in the acting of *You Never Can Tell*, one must reckon the constant flashes of Mr Shaw's verbal fireworks. It is these that form the staple of a curious and unconventional play. One cannot measure the author by the ordinary standards that prevail in the theatre. He is a thing apart, to be taken or left as the taste of the spectator may determine. But, at all events, in *You Never Can Tell* Mr Shaw gives his admirers more laughter for their money than he has done in any of his previous essays. And laughter counts for much in the playhouse just now.

John Bull's Other Island
Royal Court Theatre, 1 November 1904
Daily Telegraph, 2 November 1904

"You are so clever in your foolishness," says a character in Mr George Bernard Shaw's new play in speaking to an Englishman, "and you are so foolish in your cleverness," he says, turning to an Irishman, "that between you John Bull's other island has not got a chance." It would be to inquire too nicely—and perhaps also too rudely—if we asked into which of these categories Mr Shaw himself falls. But the fact is that whether owing to the folly of the author's cleverness or the cleverness of his folly, the "new and unpublished play" is anything but effective. It is full of good things and of happy witticisms. We always expect Mr Shaw to be mordantly clever—and we are rarely disappointed. There is a pretty episode in which an ex-priest, Keegan, has an animated dialogue with a grasshopper. There is a most original love-scene in which the Englishman, Mr Broadbent, wins the hand of the Irish maiden, Nora, by a mixture of bluster and obtuseness. Purple patches abound—especially an impassioned harangue near the close, admirably delivered by Mr Granville Barker, in the person of Mr Keegan, a passage touched with a higher eloquence than that to which Mr Shaw has accustomed us. A vigorous exposition of the aims of the Liberal party is put into the mouth of Broadbent, a brilliant bit of satire on the Liberal acceptation of the terms, Peace, Retrenchment, and Reform. And naturally there are the wonted audacities, the polished buffoonery, the farcical hysterics of Mr Shaw. A pig is taken in a motor-car, with the result that two men are thrown out, another has two of his fingers mutilated, and a considerable part of the village is reduced to ruins. We know these gallipots, as Cicero used to say. Nor would it be like our author if he did not laugh at everything and everyone, including himself. He laughs at The Tories, the Unionists, the Liberals. He laughs at Home Rule, and then, turning round, laughs at Conservative panaceas. The motto, "Efficiency," is scathingly exposed in a studied bit of oratory. The English idea of humour is derided by the Irish, and then, in its turn, the hollowness of Irish wit is tossed on points of ridicule. And now and again, as is Mr Shaw's way, graceful and tender little scenes and passages are sandwiched between great hunks of bombastic frivolity. What such a piece should be called, whether political tract, imaginative fantasia, rollicking farce, or pyrotechnic display, it would tax human ingenuity to determine. The one thing that is certain is that it is not a play. "It's all tommy rot," cries one character, "but it's devilish brilliant." "It reminds me of old Ruskin," says another. Somewhere between these two poles lies the longitude of *John Bull's Other Island*.

"My form of humbug is to tell the truth," is one of the apophthegms of Larry Doyle. Is this, too, the aim of Mr Bernard Shaw? We cannot be certain. Cleverness is a very desolating gift of humanity—most of all, perhaps, when a man assumes the cap and bells of a professional jester. For people are apt to take him at his word, and always expect him to play the fool. And then what becomes of the effort to tell the truth? In the case of *John Bull's Other Island* we can imagine one section of the audience simply regarding it as an extravaganza. Possibly, that is, indeed, the right way to take it, as assuredly it is the only way to enjoy it. Then we can laugh with a free heart, knowing full well that we shall have abundant opportunities of laughter. We will not treat Broadbent and Larry Doyle, Keegan and Patsy Farrell, Barney Doran and Matthew Haffigan, as actual personages, but only as George Bernard Shaw coined into little pieces, odd corners and fragments of the curiously analytical and sceptical intelligence of the author. But, unfortunately, another section of the audience may feel bound to accept the play differently. It may be intended as a serious contribution to the Irish problem, or a profound parable of the ascendancy of the Anglo-Saxon. From the one point of view, Mr Shaw's deliberate contribution to current politics would be an affirmation that the English and Irish, being totally different in temperament and character, never have understood, and never will understand, one another. From the other standpoint, the moral would seem to be the inevitable victory of the Anglo-Saxon type because of its masterful impenetrability to ideas. In each case, we observe, the conclusion is wholly pessimistic. Nothing will ever reconcile John Bull with his other island; it is a clear case of incompatibility of temper. The Englishman wins in the long run, on the strength of his own obtuse vigour—just because he is enterprising and stupid, a splendid, unhumorous, unintelligent animal. Mr Broadbent, in Mr Shaw's fable, has entirely the best of it. He will win over an Irish constituency, although they laugh at him; he will carry off Larry Doyle's prospective bride, Nora, although she can hardly tolerate him; he will plant a hotel and make golf links at Roscullen, even though Keegan, the dreamer, prefers the wild savagery of the landscape and a ruined round tower unrepaired by English masons. The world suffereth violence, and the violent take it by force. The Irish are infinitely more poetical and witty, and clever and imaginative. But the English prevail, owing to the victorious qualities of their efficient dulness. Whatever else Mr Shaw may do, he certainly makes us despair. We laugh with a wry face at pessimism grinning behind a comic mask. There is nothing genial, or generous, or human in Mr Shaw's mirth. In this play, which was no play, and never apparently intended to be one, there were several opportunities for good acting. Mr Louis Calvert, for instance, had admirable chances as Mr Broadbent, of which he made very good use. He had to represent a fatuous, self-satisfied Englishman, more than a little blatant and assertive, and yet to retain our sympathies, through his sheer good temper and bonhomie. In the last two acts, above all, Mr Calvert's technical skill was of the greatest value. As a matter of fact, his was the only creation of the afternoon which seemed to have some real humanity about it. Mr J.L. Shine had apparently lost his voice, and certainly had lost his memory in the representation of Larry Doyle, Broadbent's friend—a difficult, unsympathetic, and poorly written part. Other impersonations worthy of notice were those of Mr Granville Barker as Keegan, Mr Grahame Browne as Patsy Farrell, and Mr A.E. George as Matthew Haffigan. Mr Wilfred Shine drew an excellent portrait of Barney Doran, while from an amateur standpoint the performance of Miss Agnes Thomas as Aunt Judy and Miss Ellen O'Malley as Nora was something more than creditable. In the latter case, indeed, two successive scenes, first with Larry Doyle, and then with Broadbent, were carried through with remarkable skill. We cannot say, however, that the make-up of the characters was in every case a success; some of the wigs could hardly pass muster, and the piece as a whole was insufficiently rehearsed. Not that these things mattered in a matinée like this, or in a play like this. The occasion was one for intelligent amateurs, and the drama did not even begin to be dramatic. Mr George Bernard Shaw has other aims than those of pleasing an ordinary public or writing a stage play. And, after all, like his great Athenian prototype, he can be imagined to mutter, "What does Hippoclides care?"

Man and Superman
Royal Court Theatre, 23 May 1905
Daily Telegraph, 24 May 1905

Of course, the title has little or nothing to do with the play. There is no particular exposition of a Nietzschean philosophy, such as the word "superman" might suggest. Nor, indeed, is there a play at all, for, if one thinks of it, it is a strange thing that the whole of an act can be cut out of a play as originally designed, and yet do practically no harm to the story. Nor yet again are we right in calling it a story. It is a comedy of a sort, a comedy that consists of brilliant utterances, of contrasted characters, of episodes which follow one another and are not indissolubly connected to a plot, of fragments of philosophy, or rather social ethics which meet and cancel each other. There is hardly a single doctrine which Mr Shaw puts before us of which he does not also show the hollowness. Are we to believe in an ideal of free love? So Mrs Shaw's representative, Mr John Tanner, is inclined to suggest in the first act. But if so we are quickly shown that there is a great deal to be said for the ordinary and orthodox social creed. Is woman's cause to be put before us—the rights of woman, as an older generation might phrase it? If so, we are immediately confronted by an equally elegant exposition of the rights of man. And now, having delivered ourselves of these obvious and platitudinous remarks—which, after all, only amount to the assertion that we have been witnessing a play of Bernard Shaw's—let us frankly admit that it is one of the most amusing pieces of work which even the Court Theatre has ever put on the stage. The first act especially is quite admirable in the brightness of its sallies, the rapier-like touch with which foible after foible is grazed, pricked like a bubble and thrown away, the deftness of its manipulation, and the cleverness of its drawing of character. The piece does not go on as well as it opens; the second act is not as good as the first, and there are positively some passages in the third which become almost tedious. But who except Mr Shaw could give us so admirable a chauffeur as Henry Straker, so eccentric and so truthful a study of himself as Mr John Tanner, or indeed such well-written parts throughout as those which meet in the devious windings, the labyrinthian turns of *Man and Superman*?

The one thing that comes out clearly in the play is that most characteristic dogma of Mr Shaw's philosophy, which deals with the obscure and unending struggle between the sexes. According to the author of *Man and Superman*, woman is always the hunter, man is always the hunted. Ann Whitefield has marked down several quarries for destruction, and she always gets her way. She takes up Octavius Robinson as a pastime or side issue, but the great conquest of her bow and spear is the very individual who sees most clearly through her wiles, Mr John Tanner himself. Sentiment here, as always, Mr Shaw rejects with scorn. Poor little Octavius, or Ricky-ticky-tavy, Robinson, is sentimentally in love with Ann, and is made a conspicuous fool. There is no sentimentality in the relations between John Tanner and the resolute young lady, who makes herself his wife. It is all the case of the "Life-force," of the struggle of the "Will of Love," which Mr Shaw has borrowed from the philosophies of Schopenhauer and Nietzsche. Woman is a concentrated life-force, a sort of Nature personified, whose blind ends she has to carry out. Man is the helpless victim. Beyond this one clearly illuminated point, however, there is really very little to be said about *Man and Superman*. There are admirably drawn characters—Old Roebuck Ramsden, representing the Liberalism of the earlier part of the nineteenth century; John Tanner, the exemplar of modern socialistic thought; Henry Straker, a most up-to-date chauffer, with free and easy manners, and an abundance of common sense; Hector Malone, a young American, and his Irish-bred father, Mr Malone, to say nothing of the two main exponents of the Amazonian idea, Violet Robinson and Ann Whitefield. They were capitally played also. Mr Granville Barker, without whose aid Mr Shaw's plays would be even less explicable than they are, Mr J.D. Beveridge, Miss Lillah McCarthy, and Miss Sarah Brooke, were all excellent. So, too, were Mr Charles Goodhart, Mr Edmund Gwenn (the chauffeur), Miss Florence Haydon, and the rest. Whatever else Mr Shaw may do, he enables our actors and actresses to do themselves abundant justice, and that is no slight boon. It may be added, perhaps, that in this acting version of the play, the whole of the third act goes out, containing those remarkable scenes in which the Devil, Don Juan, and others expound to a reluctant and somewhat obdurate World the real philosophy of Hell.

Major Barbara
Royal Court Theatre, 28 November 1905
Daily Telegraph, 29 November 1905

MR BERNARD SHAW'S IDEAS

Whatever may be the fate of Mr Bernard Shaw's new play, *Major Barbara*, whether it ultimately turns out a success, or is acknowledged—as we think more likely—as inferior both in cleverness and dramatic skill to *John Bull's Other Island* and *Man and Superman*, there is one thing, at all events, which, for the sake of future spectators, should be done at once. The last scene in the last act should be ruthlessly shortened. When a man becomes tired, he very often drops into a verbosity which is not natural to him. Probably Mr Bernard Shaw got tired when he was half-way through the third act, and having nothing very new to say, proceeded to say a good deal more than he originally intended. The second scene in the third act drags woefully, and as it slowly works towards an end long ago foreseen, it becomes inexpressibly wearisome. The general idea of the plot may be expressed in various ways. It is the contrast between a narrow religiosity and a wide commercial outlook. Or else it is the exploding of such old prejudices as are enshrined under the name of education, morality, and religion. Or, again, put in another way, it is the inculcation of the doctrine that poverty is the most deadly of all sins, and that England is governed not by its wise, or its clever, or able, or well-educated men, but by those who have been money-grubbers all their lives, and have attained to colossal fortunes. Even yet we have hardly exhausted the possible meanings of Mr Shaw's fable. A professor of Greek has no business to be a drum beater in the Salvation Army. A girl with pure and lofty ideals of Christianity is ill-advised to become Major Barbara, and the sooner she gets out of this condition and marries a wealthy man the better for her and for society at large. Or, once more, to finish a catalogue almost as wearisome as Mr Shaw's last act, a lady like Lady Britomart Undershaft, who likes a fashionable home, and is expensive in her tastes, ought either not to separate from her low-born and wealthy husband, or, if she determines on this course, ought not to give him an opportunity of returning and spreading far and wide the doctrines of his unmitigated materialism. But whatever aspects or features the play may present to us in its diverse and often scintillating exposition, we have pretty well got to the end of our patience, and Mr Shaw has pretty well got to the end of his preaching, about the middle of the last act. To have a series of orations from Mr Undershaft, who is the millionaire, Adolphus Cusins, who is the Greek Professor, and Barbara Underhill [sic], who is the lady whom Cusins is going to marry, is quite unnecessary and otiose. In his final half-hour, Mr Shaw did his best to wipe out the clear-cut impression of the rest of the afternoon's entertainment.

What kind of entertainment it was it is unnecessary, or perhaps impossible, to say in detail. We know something about the "Shavian" method nowadays; we are always quite aware that it leads nowhere, that it is full or paradoxes, that it has a sort of desolating cleverness about it, that it is purely destructive, and never constructive. We also fully comprehend that the author himself will do his best to put before us each side of a controversy in turn, and make all the single elements of the problem mutually destructive. Others may seek a soul of goodness in things evil; it is Mr Shaw's mission to find evidences of evil in things good. [*A plot summary follows.*]

There is nothing much more to tell of the story. Numerous conversations have already explained to us that the real hero in our modern state, the real reformer, the real beneficient energy from which peace and prosperity flow, is the materialistic millionaire. When all the company visit his wonderful works they see contentment everywhere, high wages, model cottages, an ideally happy colony, with every opportunity for culture and refinement. Mr Undershaft himself makes no bones about his religious faith or his morality. He does not believe in morality. He believes in getting on, in commercial success. He does not believe in religion. He is a secularist. But he wins all along the line. He has succeeded in proving to his daughter, Barbara, that her poor, innocent Christian creed is not adapted to the conditions or the needs of a commercial state. He has proved to his wife that she cannot possibly get on without him. He has proved to his son that he is absolutely of no use in a commonwealth based on money, and may exercise his skill in the wholly unproductive and quite unnecessary departments of politics, literature, and journalism. But perhaps his greatest triumph is to have swept Mr Adolphus Cusins into his all-capacious net of sordid money-making. There are many things which Mr Bernard Shaw loves to deride. In this play he is forever tossing on points of critical scorn a knowledge of the dead languages. Really, Professor Gilbert Murray has a right to complain when Adolphus Cusins is not only described as a professor of Greek, but made up after his likeness. To beat the big drum in the Salvation Army is, perhaps, a degradation, but it is nothing compared with his final fate. He is made the heir to the Undershaft millions, and has to take his place as one of the chief workers in the great Undershaft arsenal. "Surely," remarks one of the characters, "there must be some meaning beneath all this terrible irony!" But in Major Barbara the meaning is that there is no meaning. There is nothing that we care for or respect which cannot be laughed out of court; there are no feelings, however intimate or sacred, which cannot be trampled upon; there is nothing valuable in all the hard-won exertions of thinkers and poets; the most appallingly successful industry of all is the manufacture of those arms of precision the office of which is to destroy men's lives. Such is Mr Shaw's gospel in his latest piece, bitterer and more cynical, it seems to us, than any chapter in the Shavian book of "good tidings." The only solid thing is a sort of recommendation to accept the principles of Socialism—that kind of Socialism which sneers at culture, mocks at religion, does not believe in sincere unselfishness, and has at least the merit of being likely to bring the capitalist to his senses.

Major Barbara was exceedingly well played. It is usually the good fortune, or the admirable skill, of the Bernard Shaw theatre to bring out all the best that there is in the actors and actresses who interpret it. Miss Rosina Filippi as Professor Gilbert Murray's mother-in-law—we beg pardon, as Lady Britomart Undershaft—acted with her usual fine discernment and skill. Mr Granville Barker's picture of Adolphus Cusins, the Greek professor, was excellently conceived and carried out, and Mr Louis Calvert, when he is a little more sure of his speeches, will make a good study of Andrew Undershaft, the millionaire. Miss Annie Russell, coming back to us on this side of the water after an interval of many years, obtained a triumph of sincere and restrained emotion as Barbara. But, perhaps, one of the most successful of all was the realistic and forcible Bill Walker of Mr Oswald Yorke. Stephen, the average British young man, was cleverly portrayed by Mr Hubert Harben. Miss E. Wynne-Matthison only had a small part as Mrs Baines, and Mr Edmund Gwenn, who gave us the memorable portrait of the chauffeur in *Man and Superman*, was content with the purely subordinate character of a workman among the high explosive sheds of the Undershaft business.

Captain Brassbound's Conversion
Royal Court Theatre, 20 March 1906
Daily Telegraph, 21 March 1906

MRS ELLEN TERRY

Mr Bernard Shaw must forgive us if we consider *Captain Brassbound's Conversion* as far inferior in interest to the reappearance of Miss Ellen Terry. The piece forms one of the author's so-called "Plays for Puritans." It is not nearly as good dramatically as *The Devil's Disciple*, nor is it as amusing as *Caesar and Cleopatra*. As a matter of fact, it comes within an approachable distance of dulness, especially in the first act and through half the second act. And the reason is perfectly plain. Only in the last half of the play does Lady Cecily [sic] Waynflete become of real importance. When, however, that eccentric, good-natured, and perfectly charming lady begins seriously to exercise her influence on all those surrounding her, and especially on Captain Brassbound, the play wakes up, and is genuinely interesting right up to its close. Lady Cecily Waynflete is, indeed, the only thoroughly drawn character in the piece, with the possible exception of the cockney, Felix Drinkwater. Certain it is that, as played by Miss Ellen Terry, the part is not only of relatively greater value than any other, but of almost crushing predominance. Miss Terry's performance reminds us once again—if, indeed, any reminder is necessary—that the great thing which tells on the stage, as in life, is the possession of a distinct and powerful personality. The actress opened rather uncertainly; she was never very sure of her words; but the winning charm, the clever management of her scenes, the sweetness of her smile, the easy, confident graciousness of her manner—these were the things which carried conviction in every heart. Nor must we forget that Lady Cecily has a fund of natural humour, and in giving picturesque emphasis to this side of the character Miss Terry's representation alternately reminded us of her beautiful Portia and her inimitable Beatrice. Technically, too, the performance was a remarkable one, for Lady Cecily has to manage an exceedingly difficult scene at the close—a scene which might very easily strike a wrong note. As a matter of fact, it was one of the best-played scenes of the whole. The actress has to be reasonable and engaging and persuasive and humorous all at once; she has almost to acknowledge the animal magnetism which Captain Brassbound asserts over her, and yet retain enough feminine strategy to resist. The way in which Miss Terry pronounced the final words of the play, "How glorious! How glorious! And what an escape!" was a triumphant revelation of that unique power by which, on the very eve of her professional jubilee, she yet holds her position on the stage.

As to the play itself, we perhaps need not give more than a general outline of its story. [*A plot summary follows.*]

In this piece the honours fell, as a matter of course, to Miss Ellen Terry, but there were several nice bits of characterisations besides. Mr Edmund Gwenn, whose admirable chauffeur in *Man and Superman* we are not likely to forget, had a somewhat difficult task in representing the cockney, Drinkwater, for the vernacular did not seem to come quite spontaneously from his lips. But it was a good performance, nevertheless, and one on which the actor ought to be congratulated. Mr Frederick Kerr, not perhaps very happily cast as Captain Brassbound, nevertheless represented that swashbuckler with boldness and sincerity. All his scenes with Lady Cecily were well played, but he was at his best in the final scene of renunciation. Mr J.H. Barnes was capital as Sir Howard Hallam, representing with no little skill his somewhat ponderous solemnity. Mr James Carew made an admirable American naval captain. And of the others perhaps Mr Edmund Gurney's Johnson, a prominent and burly member of Brassbound's crew, and Mr Cremlin's Rankin deserve most mention. But the piece altogether was well played, and although it can hardly be said to have captured the house, it was received with considerable applause. Miss Ellen Terry received, as was her due, an enthusiastic ovation.

The Doctor's Dilemma
Royal Court Theatre, 20 November 1906
Daily Telegraph, 21 November 1906

Mr Bernard Shaw, who is always fertile in expedients, cleverly uses a scientific and medical discovery to serve as an apology for, or introduction to, his play. In reality, he is not thinking very much of his science, albeit that so large an amount of technical phraseology runs through the piece. Far more interesting elements are combined in the latest drama than could be extracted out of the particular success or failure of Opsonin. [*The review then comments on each of the doctors' medical quackeries.*] Mr Bernard Shaw's first act is entirely occupied with these discussions, carried out with admirable humour by various parties in the controversy. It is by no means the worst of the acts; on the contrary, it has touches which, though they do not place it quite as high as the first act of *Man and Superman*, yet undoubtedly constitute a very good specimen of Mr Shaw's workmanship.

We will get rid of all this scientific framework, or rather scaffolding, for the interest in the new play assuredly does not lie in Opsonin. Its first and main interest bears relation to the author. It has sometimes been urged against Mr Bernard Shaw that he does not cultivate the virtues of the heart, but only the qualities of the head. Over and over again we have been brought to the edge of a love-scene, and found that Mr Shaw, being averse from emotional displays, had held back his hand. But if anyone supposes that our author is afraid of tenderness, let *The Doctor's Dilemma* reassure him. We have here four sketches of character which are conceived and executed with a tenderness which is quite remarkable. Old Sir Patrick Cullen, to choose a prominent example, is not only always on the side of common-sense, but is a lovable and affectionate old man. Let us remark in passing that he is also used in the play to enunciate precisely those sentiments which are the least characteristic of the author. If a daring tenet is advanced, bearing the hall-mark of modern cynicism, Sir Patrick Cullen's rejoinder is generally coined in a totally different mint. Nor does he stand alone. Dr Blenkinsop is an attractive little sketch of the general practitioner, who has steadily gone downhill through poverty and honesty. Emmy, Sir Colenso's servant, is a delightful old woman, who twists both her master and his patients around her finger, and generally secures his attention for any and every deserving case. And now comes the greatest surprise of all. For once, Mr Shaw has drawn a loving woman. Jennifer Dubedat is more even than that; she loves her husband, the worthless Louis Dubedat, and not only with that unreasoning affection which makes him secure in all his selfishness, but with a whole-hearted admiration for his genius and a triumphant determination to vindicate his memory, which lift her into a wholly new category of Mr Shaw's women. If Jennifer is a surprise because she is so loyal and so human, Louis Dubedat is equally a surprise, because, though he is intended to be a decisive example of an artistic temperament, he somehow fails to convince. He utters, of course, the kind of remarks which no doubt belong to men who feel the inspiration of art and make it a substitute for morality, but something more than that is required to convert him into a veritably life-like figure, and it is, unfortunately, the something more which is not always given to us.

[*The review then gives a plot and character summary, singling out Sir Colenso Ridgeon as an example of Shaw the "masterly psychologist."*] For Sir Colenso is absolutely real, exceedingly human in his weakness and in his strength, not merely an abstract medical authority, but a concrete man of ordinary flesh and blood, easily tempted, and often mistaking his very temptations for virtues. Indeed, Sir Colenso is the best-drawn figure in the piece, and it was played by Mr Ben Webster in a fashion which that actor has rarely, if ever, equalled. Mr Ben Webster's young men we know; with Mr Ben Webster's middle-aged men we have hitherto made no acquaintance. We only hope that he will give us some more studies of this kind, so capitally conceived and so intelligently executed. It was a fine part to play, and it is not too much to say that Mr Webster played it finely.

Meanwhile, the story runs on to its inevitable conclusion. In the incompetent hands of Sir Ralph Bonnington, Louis Dubedat dies, and we have a very harrowing death scene on the stage, in which the artist, being wheeled into his own studio, describes to us in graphic terms the objects of his artistic creed, and utters his last word, pillowed against his wife's bosom. The scene was pathetic and almost tragic, and coming, as it did, towards the conclusion of a play which had been to a large extent farcical in character, its sheer unconventionality produced a decided shock. Nor did Mr Shaw spare us one atom of the horror of the incident. He puts into the mouth of the dying man a sort of creed: "I believe in Michael Angelo and Velasquez. I believe in the Gospel of Beautiful Colour," and so forth, in flagrant bad taste—as it seems to the present writer—and if intended to vindicate the artistic conscience, a curious failure. However, he dies artistically, at all events, and consistently with the manner in which throughout he has been drawn—a person labelled as an artist, and existing for the utterance of so-called artistic sentiments, but a shallow thing at best, a bloodless phantom, a mere creature of Mr Shaw's whimsical mind, with little power to arrest or interest. Then after the death scene we get an epilogue, quite one of the happiest features of the production. [*The scene is described.*] So ends a play which is at once remarkable and significant, not because it satirises the doctors, not because it attempts to reveal the psychology of the artist, but because it puts before us a dramatist who can draw a vivid and true character in Sir Colenso, and a loving woman in Jennifer Dubedat. For the rest, of course, we have the usual signs and evidences by which we recognise the author's work. He always supplies a corrective to any and every opinion which is advanced by his personages; or, if we like to phrase it so, gives poison and antidote with impartial hand. He introduces a vulgar newspaper man into the death scene, with his note-book and his greedy rapacity for news. He spoils a rather touching death scene with an extraordinary burlesque of greed. He introduces an amazing farrago of Shakesperian quotations, which he puts in the mouth of Sir Ralph, the humbug. And, in a fashion that seems to be growing on him more and more in every production, he appears totally unable to keep the name of George Bernard Shaw out of his play. We know some of these tricks of old; without them, indeed, we should hardly recognise the writer. They make spectators laugh, and that is their sole justification. But what it would be absurd not to recognise in *The Doctor's Dilemma* is a decided advance in firmness and decision in Mr Shaw's characterisation, and a greater attention than it is his wont to pay to the process of construction. *The Doctor's Dilemma* is not a mere entertainment, as were *John Bull's Other Island* and *Man and Superman*, but a real play.

It was acted with vigorous and discriminative skill to which it would be difficult to give too much praise. Mr William Farren, jun., gave the right senile and sensible touches to Sir Patrick Cullen. Mr James Earn was an admirable Cutler Walpole, a surgeon in manner as well as in speech, and Mr Granville Barker, by his versatile art, lent an interest to Louis Dubedat, which, so far as we can discover, did not reside in the part itself. Mr Eric Lewis triumphantly exhibited all the foibles, the rodomontade, the endless commonplaces of that imperfectly-equipped doctor, Sir Ralph Bloomfield Bonington. It was an exceedingly clever performance, although it so far accentuated the farcical elements as to make it a little difficult to believe in the individuality. But doubtless Sir Ralph exists for a farcical purpose, so that the actor was justified in his interpretation. There remain several other interpretations to which, if we had space, we would gladly refer. We must content ourselves, however, by saying that Miss Lillah McCarthy, when she got her chance in the fourth act and in the epilogue, played with no little power and dignity, and that Miss Clare Greet gave due distinction to the amiable humours of Emmy. The piece was received, of course, with sympathy and interest, but we are bound to confess that during and after the death scene some of the interest of the spectators seemed to evaporate. *The Doctor's Dilemma* will still bear compression, for it played for three hours and a half—rather a long space of time to give in our modern world to any play.

Don Juan in Hell
Royal Court Theatre, 4 June 1907
Daily Telegraph, 5 June 1907

Phew! What an afternoon! The entertainment began at 2.30 and ended at 5.30 [*a double-bill of* Don Juan in Hell *followed by* The Man of Destiny]. Three solid hours of George Bernard Shaw—and not Mr Shaw at his best—was a burden which the audience found it exceedingly difficult to bear. The first piece, *Don Juan in Hell*, which is the omitted third act of *Man and Superman*, is a long and rambling philosophical treatise on many subjects, carried on at almost interminable length by the Devil, the Commander, Dona Ana, and Don Juan himself. Of course, it is not a play, nor anything approaching to one; it is a discussion, a debate, a dialogue, a conference, a sermon—anything and everything that is long-winded and solemn, lit, it is true, with occasional glimpses of wit, but without much humour. It is probably wrong to imagine that Mr Shaw is a humorous man. He has abundance of wit, sometime exceedingly bright and vivacious, as in the first act of *Man and Superman*, and through many of the acts of *John Bull's Other Island*. But the worst of him is that he is so deadly in earnest. He is exceedingly serious about his own theories, and, as is usually the case, the determined and obstinate prophet is not remarkable for his sense of humour. [. . .]

There was one exceedingly wonderful thing in *Don Juan in Hell*, but it had nothing to do either with the author or the piece. It was the extraordinary memory possessed by Mr Robert Loraine and Mr Norman McKinnel, which enabled these clever actors to repeat some miles of windy metaphysics without the loss of a word. Anything better than Mr Robert Loraine's performance in this respect we have never seen. He makes, we understand, a charming and most successful John Tanner; he certainly makes a charming and most successful Don Juan Tenorio. And Mr Norman McKinnel only comes second. The part of the Devil is not a remarkably good one in Mr Shaw's version, for, as Don Juan remarks, one can learn something from a cynical Devil, but it is difficult to endure a sentimental one. Yet Mr McKinnel did wonders with his materials. To him is given one of the longest speeches that could be found in any play, and he said it without a single fault. The other personages involved in the discussion—for we entirely refuse to call it a drama—also did excellently well. Miss Lillah McCarthy looked fascinating in a large crinoline, and as for Mr Michael Sherbrooke as the Statue of the Commander, he was of priceless service to the piece, from his delightfully clear and crisp utterance. Moreover, *Don Juan* was cleverly put upon the stage. The lights, put in front of the proscenium, not behind it, made it possible to have a dead black velvet background, against which the characters, dressed in colours, stood out admirably. Everything was carefully thought out which could help the illusion; everything excellently devised—except the piece itself. We do not object to it as a metaphysical discussion, bien entendu; we only quarrel with its pretensions to be called a play. [*There follows a summary of the main ideas of the play.*] For the rest, the piece discusses the meaning of the life-force and the secret aims of Nature in providing mankind with a brain, in a fashion with which any of those whose melancholy duty it has been to peruse modern German philosophy will be perfectly familiar. Begin with Kant, with his belief in the Thing-in-itself; go on to Schopenhauer, with his Will to Live; and with Nietzsche and his Superman—and you have the keynotes of Mr Shaw's *Don Juan in Hell*. You have also the advantage of reading about these things in books, safely ensconced in an armchair in a study. You have not got the ill-luck to see them labelled as a drama and placed in all their naked sophistry on the stage. [. . .]

Amongst other wonderful things in this wonderful afternoon was the sublime patience of the audience. They admired, as indeed they ought to have admired, the easy naturalness and marvellous memory of the actors and actresses, and they gave both pieces the reward of their generous applause. And yet some of them must have been bored almost to tears.

The Devil's Disciple
Savoy Theatre, 14 October 1907
Daily Telegraph, 15 October 1907

It is written by Bernard Shaw himself—and who shall dispute an author's right to pronounce judgment on his own work?—that *The Devil's Disciple* is sheer melodrama. There is, on his own confession, hardly an incident in this piece which every old patron of the Adelphi pit would not recognise as a familiar and highly-prized friend. Which of these old playgoers, indeed, would refuse a kindly welcome to such well-established devices as the reading of the will in the first act, of the oppressed orphan finding a protector, of the arrest, the heroic sacrifice, the court-martial, the scaffold, and the reprieve at the last moment? Are not those things, Mr Shaw urges, as easily and as readily recognised as the beefsteak pudding on the bill of fare at every restaurant? What beneficent influence, then—we are still quoting Mr Shaw—was brought to bear upon the play to secure for it in America a chorus of enthusiastic praise raised in honour of its novelty, of an originality that almost bordered upon the confines of audacious eccentricity? A less candid writer would probably have kept the truth to himself, would have hidden it away as a secret, the disclosure of which might well serve to injure his reputation. Not Mr Shaw, however. Openly and unhesitatingly he has made it known that the American public failed to discover the hackneyed elements in *The Devil's Disciple* because it was blinded, er—should we not say, rather, deafened?—by "my trumpet and cartwheel declamation." The recognition of original work in England is, it would appear, of slower growth, the only cure for this unfortunate state of affairs being "sedulous advertisement." And, acting upon this principle, Mr Shaw tells us in his elaborate preface to *The Devil's Disciple* wherein lies the true novelty of the play. That is to be found in the character of the hero, a young Puritan who, starved of religion—the most clamorous need of his nature—abruptly turns in a diametrically opposite direction, takes Hatred instead of Pity for his master-passion, compassionates the devil and champions him, and ends by becoming, like all truly religious men, a reprobate and an outcast. Once this is understood, it is Mr Shaw who again speaks, "the play becomes straightforwardly simple."

With these facts in their possession, it is clearly the fault of the public, and the public alone, if they misunderstand the inwardness and the significance of the piece presented last night at the Savoy Theatre. But whatever saving grace it may have in the shape of a subtle and elusive psychology, we are still constrained to describe it as melodrama tempered by exuberant farce. We write under the possibility of correction by the author, but unless we are much mistaken, *The Devil's Disciple* was the outcome of a commission given to Mr Shaw by the late

William Terriss in the days when he ruled over the dominion of the Adelphi. It is easy to imagine that eminently robust actor's feelings of blank astonishment and horror when he came to study the part of Dick Dudgeon. No hero this assuredly, but a man condemned out of his own mouth of impulses and of a nature peculiar to the meanest type of humanity. But hardly have we time to place Dick in his ignoble niche than behold! the amazing fellow performs the paradoxical feat of rushing to the rescue of a stranger, an individual for whom he has the heartiest contempt, and of offering to sacrifice his own life in order to secure the other's safety. Marvelling greatly, we ask ourselves why? It is at this point that our gentle cicerone, Mr Shaw, once more steps in to enlighten us. Men, he contends, are not, save on the stage, subject to the governing force of reason. They do things simply because they have to be done; the opportunity is there, and they cannot resist seizing upon it. So it is with Dick Dudgeon. It would have been the simplest thing in the world to have made of him another Sidney Carton, to have brought him to the scaffold fired with an ambition to restore the woman he loves to the arms of her devoted husband. But this is not Mr Shaw's way. Dick Dudgeon's actions shall smack of the rankest heroism, but at heart he is merely a dissolute dare-devil, with a keen sense of the irony that permeates life from first to last. Regard him in any other light and the play becomes a distorted and shapeless mess, without meaning or significance.

[*There follows a plot summary characterizing the narrative as a trajectory from pure melodrama to a "descent" into farce.*]

Perhaps some of us are tempted to think that the author has not dealt quite fairly with his audience, that, as on so many other occasions, he has played upon their feelings only to laugh at their weakness in allowing these to be harrowed. The insincerity of such behaviour is incontestable, and apparently no one suffered from it last night more than the performers themselves. That they felt doubtful as to the manner in which the piece should be handled was clear throughout. Lightning flashes of melodrama across a comedy sky could be discovered at every instant. The strenuous method of Miss Bateman [Mrs Dudgeon] had little in common with the subdued note struck by Miss Wynne Matthison [Judith Anderson] or the quiet suavity and mediocrity of Mr Granville Barker's General Burgoyne. Mr Matheson Lang's Dick Dudgeon possessed unquestionable merits. His acting was conspicuous for its earnest, manly, and forcible qualities. But it lacked something of that spirit of imaginativeness, fantastic devilry, and brilliancy that alone could make the character comprehensible. Two little character sketches deserve, on the other hand, all praise, namely the sergeant of Mr Kenyon Musgrave and the Essie of Miss Marjorie Day. In the role of Anderson Mr C. Rann Kennedy, when he succeeded in shaking off his nervousness, played, too, with great vigour and intensity. As a whole, however, the performance wanted homogeneity, and treatment of that robust order necessary to the well-being alike of melodrama and of farce. Let the Savoy company look to it. There is no lack of material in *The Devil's Disciple* to work upon, but it is material that must not be approached with kid gloves on hands. The methods which suited the Court Theatre may very well be found inadequate and out of place at the Savoy.

Caesar and Cleopatra
Savoy Theatre, 25 November 1907
Daily Telegraph, 26 November 1907

Like Audrey's bucolic charm, as criticised by Touchstone, Mr Shaw's *Caesar and Cleopatra* is "not for all markets." Some might find it a little bitter to the taste, as though the author of the piece were laughing at us for spurious Caesar-worship; others, discovering that they were invited to witness a sort of pantomime, might complain that the fun was not sufficiently boisterous. The spirit of the play is, indeed, a little arid and bleak. Caesar as a middle-aged rhetorician, and Cleopatra as a spiteful little vixen, do not at once commend themselves to the historic sense. But it is wrong to imagine that Mr Shaw has his tongue in his cheek. He is generally serious, and as a reformer of our politics and our morality he is in more deadly earnest than our most advanced politicians. Observe that *Caesar and Cleopatra* is one of the so-called *Plays for Puritans*, bearing company with *The Devil's Disciple* and *Captain Brassbound's Conversion*. Of all the plays for Puritans there is one characteristic quality to be noted. They never deal with romance, and, therefore, they never call up a single blush on the Nonconformist visage. Romance, sentiment? No—that is what has ruined all the British drama for years past. We are always requiring that our hero should be a real hero, magnanimous, large-hearted, and loving. We perpetually ask that the heroine and hero should be sentimentally united by bonds which owe their stringency to a capacious heart. And as all love-making is emotional and sexual, a play for Puritans shall have none of it. Mr Shaw's Egyptian play must have nothing in common with Shakespeare's *Antony and Cleopatra*, with its magnificent lyrical outbursts of human passion. As compromise for the emotion it lacks, it shall have wit, sarcasm, bombastic eloquence, elaborate fooling—what you will. It shall show you an ancient Briton gushing modern moral sentiments, and you must laugh; a child-monarch—Ptolemy XIV—who forgets his dignified set speech, and has to be prompted, and you must laugh; a nurse, endowed with a comic name, something between a sneeze and a stutter, and you must laugh; a Caesar who was annoyed at being considered old and bald, and you must laugh; a Cleopatra who is a coward and a bully and a fascinating little minx, all in one, and you must laugh. But what the dramatist at all costs must prevent is the seemingly inevitable love-scene between middle-aged hero and sixteen-year-old heroine. It is a play for Puritans. But, oh, the trouble Mr Shaw is forced to take in order that he may keep us off the emotional ground! For five long acts—or rather four, for in the present version the third act is omitted—we are perpetually trembling on the edge of a romance and perpetually being warned away. So there is nothing for it but to laugh—in order to prove that both we ourselves and the two main characters are heart-whole.

The worst of it is that though we begin with the best intentions in the world, we cannot go on laughing through four or five acts. We recognise early, of course, that *Caesar and Cleopatra* is a burlesque parody of a musical pattern—something like *Orphée aux Enfers*, or *La Belle Héloïse*, or Disraeli's *Ixion*. In that case the fun must be fairly consistent, and it must be sedulously kept up. If it is a burlesque, it must be not only comic, but hilariously comic. If it is pantomimic history, Mr Shaw must go on with unwearying zeal grinning at us through a horse-collar to the end of the story, adding jest to jest and parody to parody. Naturally, Mr Shaw, being a keenly intellectual man, declines to do anything of the sort. He begins with magnificent brio. There is Cleopatra lying between the paws of the Sphinx in the desert, and Caesar making orations to infinitude around the base of the statue. But after a time we touch a deeper note. We discover that our author is drawing for us an ideal man, a kind of Over-man, a Nietschean [sic] hero, and also, incidentally, illustrating some chapters on the education of kings. Or else, we graze the edges of melodrama. We get a scene in which through Cleopatra's machinations a man is murdered, and in revenge a woman is murdered—no less a person than the redoubtable Ftatateeta. Our burlesque standpoint has disappeared; our pantomimic history has become suddenly serious stuff. Verily, you can expel nature "with a pitchfork," but it will always return. You exclude sentiment and you get melodrama. You will not write anything but a comic satire on love-scenes, and you can relapse on murders. Caesar may be inhuman, Cleopatra inhuman, and the whole play inhuman, or, if the description be preferred, aridly intellectual and undeniably witty. But in that case, to make a play at all, you must eventually borrow from an inferior level of dramatic artifice. You must show a dead body on the stage.

It is all very clever, of course, with immense spirit and humour and "go"—a piece at which you often chuckle to yourself with suppressed and enjoyable laughter. But it is not a play on the level of *The Devil's Disciple*, or *Candida*, or *John Bull's Other Island*. It is a "tour de force" of audacity and the mocking spirit, in which the characters, for the most part, speak and think and move in the spirit of George Bernard Shaw. Last night it was very finely played, both by Mr Forbes Robertson, in the part of Caesar, and by Miss Gertrude Elliott in that of Cleopatra. Mr Roberston was dignified, incisive, humorous, full of resource and of sonorous—sometimes too sonorous—eloquence. He looked like Dante—a self-conscious rather than an inspired Dante, as indeed Mr Shaw has drawn the character. As for Miss Elliott, we have rarely seen her to greater advantage; her Egyptian queen was to the manner born, formed veritably in the Shavian mold, an admirable impersonation. Many of the others, too, did well, especially Mr Ian Robertson as Britannus and Mr Percy Rhodes as Rufio, Caesar's lieutenant. The play was received with great cordiality, Mr Robertson and Miss Elliott being welcomed enthusiastically.

Everyone is glad to see them once more on this side of the Atlantic.

Getting Married
Haymarket Theatre, 12 May 1908
Daily Telegraph, 13 May 1908

MR SHAW'S "CONVERSATION"
PARADOX AND PROLIXITY

Mr Shaw knows himself and his own qualities so well that it becomes a work of supererogation to attempt to point him or them out. He does not care to write a drama so much as to compose a species of Socratic dialogue, in which various points are taken up by various speakers, and the general conclusion is delightfully uncertain and vague. Although he often can draw character, and, according to many feminine critics, is intimately acquainted with the secrets of women's hearts, he sometimes perversely does not choose to do anything else except make all his characters talk the same language as Shaw. He is absolutely disconcerting, and he glories in the fact. He takes current notions of morality, turns them upside down, analyses them with bitter logic, and is satisfied if the result is paradoxical and annoying. Mr Shaw has told us these charming eccentricities in himself over and over again, and it is our own fault if we do not know what to expect. In *Getting Married* such characteristics meet us at every turn, with the addition, perhaps, of one which, as a clever man, Mr Shaw ought to be able to avoid. Prolixity is gaining upon him. The very facility with which he seems to talk brings with it its own temptation. His plays are over before he will permit the curtain to be rung down, and the feeling with which the majority of the audience must have left the Haymarket Theatre yesterday was probably a certain unescapeable weariness, caused by unending glitter and interminable conversation.

It is a pity, because for one hour *Getting Married* is exceedingly bright and amusing, and even for two hours the interest is kept up with no small measure of success. But then comes the fatal third act—a curious and disappointing act, which chills our interest and sends us out of the theatre a little perplexed and more than a little bored. *Getting Married* consists of three acts, with no real divisions other than the purely formal ones of raising and letting down the curtain, and played yesterday from half-past two till half-past five. If we ask what it was all about, it is easy to give a general answer, but very difficult to give an answer in detail. [*A plot summary follows.*]

In the first act all the characters talk delightfully, with the cleverness which we expect from the author, and talk, also, from an individual standpoint, carefully differentiated by their different personalities. At the end of the first act everyone was amused and delighted. There was quite sufficient dramatic interest on the stage to arouse attention, and it looked as if the inter-action of these characters was going to help on the process of the drama. But then came the disappointment. As the play proceeded much of the individuality seemed to be dropped. We approximated more and more to the usual standpoint of Mr Bernard Shaw, and instead of the dialogue leading on to definite points and issues, it lost itself in a morass of wearisome epigrams. Some of the personages remained individual throughout. The Bishop was one, and St John Hotchkiss (a delightfully fresh character) was another. Nevertheless, we felt at the end of the second act that we had not advanced very much further than the point reached at the end of the first act, and our final expectations rested on the figure of Mrs George Collins, who makes a fine and striking entrance just before the second curtain descends. Alas! our hopes in this respect were to a large extent to be frustrated. Mrs George Collins's duty was, through her experience, to put everything right. She was to have separate interviews with the ladies and with the gentlemen and help them in their respective troubles. She does nothing of the kind. She has a flirtation with St John Hotchkiss, which ends in her own discomfiture. She reveals to the Bishop the fact that she is the fair "Incognita" who had written to him wonderfully moving love letters. And, finally, she does her best to tempt Father Anthony, on the ground that she is a woman whom no man can resist. But as to the solution of the problem of matrimony, for which she was originally intended, she does not help us a jot, until, in sudden and abrupt fashion, she becomes a hypnotised medium, an inspired prophetess, a mixture of saint, demon and pythoness, delivering herself of a long and eloquent speech, which bears little or no relation to the rest of the play. The passage to which we have just referred was in every sense disconcerting, because it was not led up to in Mr Shaw's usual felicitous fashion. But such as it was, it was the one definite utterance, the one bit of veritable gospel which our author allowed us.

What is Mr Shaw's gospel on the subject of matrimony? He voices, of course, the existing discontent. He puts plainly before us the reasons which lead one woman to refuse marriage altogether, another woman to desire to have children without having a husband, a third woman to make the discovery that she wants at least two husbands, one for Sundays and one for every day. He discusses in an amusing scene whether it would be possible to arrange matrimony as a terminable contract, and suggests that such a solution à la Meredith is impracticable, because no one could even begin to formulate the conditions. All these things merely belong to Mr Shaw as representing throughout a modern and inquiring attitude. But then comes suddenly the utterance of Mrs George Collins, a spirited and whole-hearted advocacy of what a woman demands, of the minimum with which she ought to be satisfied in the marriage state. She is called the inspirer of men's thoughts, the better genius which helps their relatively unformed characters to expand. She is the fairy godmother, who converts an ordinary house into a king's palace. She is the good angel who forgives and reconciles and spreads peace. If this be so— and the facts are recognised in the emotional utterances of many men—do not let us make her into a drudge, a slave, a merely ordinary housewife. Man must get out of the habit of demanding as his right certain things which he expects from his wife, whether physically or socially. The graciousness of her presence must be acknowledged, the independence of her person scrupulously preserved. That, so far as we can gather, is Mr Shaw's gospel of matrimony, and all his obiter dicta on the subject are just sidelights, revealing odd traits, both of men and of women, in reference to the central theme. Some women may be naturally polyandrous; all men are probably naturally inclined to polygamy. But in matrimony, as in other matters, it is the ideal which keeps things sane— it is the letter which kills, and the spirit which gives life.

It only remains to say that *Getting Married* was admirably acted by artists who did their best, and gave their utmost intelligence to the execution of Mr Shaw's projects. Miss Mary Rorke as Mrs Bridgenorth, Mr E. Holman Clark as Alderman William Collins, the greengrocer, Mr Charles Fulton as the sentimental General Bridgenorth, Miss Beryl Faber as Lesbia Grantham, Mr William Farren, jun., as Reginald Bridgenorth, and Miss Marie Löhr as Mrs Reginald gave delightful sketches of character, which were warmly appreciated by the audience. Mr Henry Ainley's Bishop was quite one of the best things of the afternoon, a suave, dignified, charming performance; while Mr Robert Loraine acted with conspicuous cleverness as St John Hotchkiss, and Miss Auriol Lee depicted Edith Bridgenorth, the recalcitrant bride, with a nice sense of character. Mr James Hearn, as Father Anthony, contributed another good impersonation, while Miss Fanny Brough, as Mrs George Collins, was, of course, a tower of strength. One of the most difficult scenes in the play was entrusted to her, when she was supposed to be in a mediumistic trance and the Bishop and Father Anthony were listening to her inspired eloquence. No one except an accomplished actress could have got through the strange scene with such success. For two acts, at all events, *Getting Married* both amused and interested the audience, but the third act, and especially the concluding portion, proved a little wearisome. The play as a whole is a characteristic piece of work. [. . .]

The Admirable Bashville
His Majesty's Theatre, 26 January 1909
Daily Telegraph, 27 January 1909

Mr Pickwick, it is recorded, envied the ease with which the friends of Mr Peter Magnus were amused. It was, no doubt, for Mr Magnus's friends that Mr Bernard Shaw wrote *The Admirable Bashville*. Others can hardly be advised to go and see it. The "masterpiece" (Mr Shaw gave it that name) was produced some years ago at the Imperial Theatre, and has, of course, been published. Those who are not familiar with it may best get a notion of its general effect from a brief account of some of the incidents. A clock strikes ten. The hero says "Hark!" ten times over, and having thus produced an iambic line, remarks, "It strikes in poetry." A footman makes the hero's nose bleed, and he is constrained to ask the heroine to "lend him a key or other frigid object." The footman, in an agony of declamation, clasps his brow, and the powder rises from his hair in clouds. Mr Sass and Mr Ben Webster fight a burlesque boxing-match. An actress describes the death of her husband in these lines: he

> After three months of wedded happiness
> Rashly fordid himself with prussic acid,
> Leaving a tear-stained note to testify
> That, having sweetly honeymooned with me,
> He now could say, O Death, where is thy sting?

Of course those who want to laugh at this sort of thing will find that the Afternoon Theatre gives them plenty to laugh at. But it seems a pity that it should not do something better. The demand for elementary humour is surely abundantly supplied already. We all know the story of the foreign attaché who, after being conducted over one of the disastrous battlefields of South Africa turned to the staff officer his guide and said, "Sir, was there no other road?" The directors of the Afternoon Theatre must have had other plays before them. There are several to Mr Shaw's name which we should have been glad to welcome again. The admirable little piece of work by George Paston [*Tilda's New Hat*], which was the second part of the performance yesterday, is evidence of what can be found by the discerning eye.

BURLESQUE AND EARNEST

When the depressing effect of the humours of *The Admirable Bashville* has in some degree abated, it is possible to remember that, like everything Mr Shaw writes, it has moments of vigour, strong rhetoric, and challenging thought. But the process of turning its original, that crude and brilliant novel, *Cashel Byron's Profession*, into a burlesque of Elizabethan drama, was disastrous. A burlesque of something or other, no doubt, *The Admirable Bashville* is, but rather of [Edward Bulwer-Lytton's] *The Lady of Lyons*, of modern melodrama, of Englishmen in general and stage tricks in particular, than anything Elizabethan. Mr Shaw has told us that it is written in blank verse. There are some speeches in it, not burlesque at all but of high seriousness, in which he has written ringing rhetorical lines. Such may be found in Cashel Byron's invective against modern civilization and Cetewayo's denunciation of England. It is in these scenes, with their fine fanatical onslaught on our society as by law and convention established, that *The Admirable Bashville* makes its only important claim to interest. They say nothing which in this year of grace sounds very new, but the reasoned passion of them is not to be forgotten. One scene more is worth recording, that of the footman's bombastic soliloquy "'Ich dien.' Damnation! I serve. My motto should have been, 'I scalp,'" and so on. This is alive with real human humour in the fantastic key. But for this scanty allowance of bread there is a monstrous deal of watery sack. The greater part of the play is, of course, not blank verse at all, except in the sense that the dull iambic rhythm which we all occasionally perpetrate when writing in haste and blot at our leisure may be called blank verse. Scraps of quotation are adapted in this style.

> This is the face that burnt a thousand boats,
> And ravished Cashel Byron from the ring.

No doubt much of the verse is believed to be a parody of Elizabethan rhythms and phrases. Some delightful work might be done in that kind, but *The Admirable Bashville* only proves that Mr Shaw is not the man to do it.

[*A brief plot summary follows.*]

FINE ACTING

For the acting there should be nothing but praise. What *The Admirable Bashville* would be like without Mr Ben Webster we should prefer not to speculate. He marched triumphantly through the mock heroics of the prize fighter, took the humours with a proper bombastic earnestness which did the best for them that could be done, and in the scenes of invective was supreme. After him equal honours belong to Mr James Hearn's dignified Cetewayo and Mr Henry Ainley's delightful footman, humorous in every detail of action, and magnificent in declamation. It is unnecessary to say that Miss Marie Löhr looked charming as the heroine [Lydia] or to add that she did all that the most humorous earnestness could do for the part. Mr Lennox Pawle's own humour was welcome as the character of the trainer [Mellish].

The programme made the alarming statement that "all the scenes will be presented simultaneously," and added that "the traditions of the Elizabethan stage will be more or less strictly adhered to in the representation of the play." [The programme note is printed in full in Shaw, *Collected Plays* 2:487-88.] This meant that there was a stage upon the stage. The smaller was used for interiors, the larger for the open air. The curtains of the smaller were in the first act drawn, and formed the background of the scene upon which two beefeaters advanced bearing a printed card which informed us where we were supposed to be. In similar style, the traditional uses of limelight and incidental music were burlesqued, and no doubt those who have never seen a pantomime or who number Mr Peter Magnus among their friends will be much amused.

Misalliance
Duke of York's Theatre, 23 February 1910
Daily Telegraph, 24 February 1910

DEBATE BY G.B. SHAW

The Repertory Theatre, which opened its doors with the grimmest of tragedies, produced as its second performance the flimsiest and airiest of Mr Shaw's thaumaturgic displays. It is very difficult to say what *Misalliance* is about; it touches on so many subjects. But there are several things which may in a limitative or negative fashion define it. It is not a play, but a conversation. It is arbitrarily divided into three parts, but there is no reason in the nature of things why it should have begun in the fashion it did, or why, having begun, it should ever have finished. It has one, or perhaps two, incidents occurring in the three hours it lasts. The first is the arrival of an aeroplane which crashes into a greenhouse, and so begins the so-called second act. The other event is the arrival of a clerk armed with a pistol, to threaten the life of Mr John Tarleton, the famous maker of unshrinkable underwear. And that commences the third division. Or we may attempt to explain the purport of *Misalliance* by its characters, despite the fact that they are very loosely related. Well, there is John Tarleton, senior, already alluded to, who is a great reader of books, and is always referring us to his literary authorities. Bentley Saumarez [*sic*] is an unlicked and effeminate cub. His father, Lord Saumarez, has ruled an Indian province—at least, that is what we are told, though from his conduct in the play we find it hard to believe it. Hypathia [*sic*] Tarleton is one of the most dreadful specimens of modern emancipated young women we have ever encountered on the stage. Mrs Tarleton, as impersonated by Miss Florence Haydon, is, of course, a dear. Besides these figures, there are John Tarleton, junior, and Joseph Percival, athletic young men; Julius Baker, apparently designed to serve as a parody on the Socialist orator, especially as he orates in Hyde Park; and last, but not least, a Polish acrobatic lady, who arrives in the aeroplane, Lina Szczepanowska, who juggles with billiard-balls and oranges, and calls John Tarleton "old pal."

INDISCRIMINATE CHATTER

Clearly, characters like these, so oddly brought into momentary unity, can give little idea of Mr Bernard Shaw's "play." Shall we try, then, another method, and catalogue some of the subjects of discussion? What did these people talk about? The title *Misalliance* suggests that they debated marriage, and certainly this was a recurrent theme. Hypathia, who has been wooed by the elderly Lord Saumarez, is, when the play opens, engaged to the young cub Bentley, and when the curtain falls on the last act, has persuaded her father to "buy the beast" (that is, Joseph Percival) for her for fifteen hundred a year. Then there is a good deal of chatter about the relations of fathers and children; the impossibility of anything save a sort of armed neutrality; the natural antagonism, as it were, between those who have lived and those who are beginning to live their lives. Of course, the aristocracy comes in for its share of Shavian satire. The only topic on which duchesses and marchionesses habitually wax eloquent is, apparently, "systems of drainage," which dear old Mrs Tarleton considers indecent, and the state of their interiors, which strikes the wife of the underclothing merchant as frankly outrageous. Sour milk naturally makes an appearance in the discussion, and the superiority of mongrels to the pure-bred—whether in dogs or men; and, strangely enough, the Bible crops up again and again, either as a book which is never read, or as containing—such is our author's benignant attitude—better literature than a halfpenny newspaper. Democracy is a pretty frequent subject—democracy to be laughed at; democracy as "reading better than it acts," like some plays; democratic Socialism, as affording material for hustings oratory, especially when the tongue is loosed with sloe-gin. We really do not know that we need refer to other matters in the prodigal and often tedious budget of debatable topics which Mr Shaw gives us. All the personages talk, and some of them talk well, while others are deadly bores. The Polish lady with the unpronounceable name talks less than any others, and perhaps for that very reason is to be preferred to all. But we ought to add that she is represented by Miss Lena Ashwell, which may have something to do with it.

UNPLEASANT CHARACTERS

One feature of the entertainment it is difficult to pass over. Whether the talk is humorous or verbose, whether the epigrams are sharp or blunt, whether the conversation on the whole is clever or dreary—and we are inclined to think that, to use one of Mr Shaw's happiest adjectives, it is "linen-draperish"—the drawing of some of the characters is almost repulsive. Bentley Saumarez, a scion of aristocracy, is a hysterical and epileptic ass. So in a somewhat different sense is Julius Baker, a clerk who spouts Socialism on 20s a week. Joseph Percival, the athletic young Apollo, is a mercenary and materialistic cad. Lord Saumarez, of course, exposes the methods of "prancing proconsul," when he has to rule natives by force or fraud. But the worst of all is the unspeakable Hypathia. She is cynical and shameless, a hunter of men, or she would not be a Shavian heroine, a tomboy of a peculiarly unpleasant type, a mannerless modern hoyden and minx, who believes herself qualified to talk on all subjects, and is under no allusion [sic] as to what she is pleased to call her heart. There are only two fairly sympathetic characters, besides Mrs Tarleton, in whom we can take a faint interest. One is John Tarleton, senior, who is amusing and quite likeable. The other is Lina Szcz—we cannot get any "forrader" with her name—who knows that physical exercise is the best cure for mental and physical hysteria. Various actors struggled to give bodily shape to these talking machines, and, on the whole, succeeded very fairly. Mr C.M. Lowne did justice to John Tarleton; Miss Lena Ashwell gave charm to the Polish lady; Mr Charles Bryant was manly and vigorous as Joseph Percival. Mr Frederick Lloyd [John Tarleton, junior], Mr Donald Calthrop [Bentley Summerhays], Miss Miriam Lewes [Hypatia Tarleton], Miss Florence Haydon [Mrs Tarleton], Mr Hubert Harben [Lord Summerhays], and Mr O.P. Heggie [Julius Baker]—the last-named in a clever sketch—completed the cast. The "debate" was received with a good deal of laughter and applause, and seemed to please the house.

Fanny's First Play
Little Theatre, 19 April 1911
Daily Telegraph, 20 April 1911

It is a very good joke when at last you get to the heart of it, which, to speak as frankly as the circumstances demand, takes some little time. *Fanny's First Play* is a satirical skit upon Shavian methods, Shavian principles, Shavian ideas, and might well have been—probably was—written by the author of *Arms and the Man* himself. Here, in short, is a clear sense of "Aut Shaw, aut Diabolus" [Either Shaw or the Devil]. In every line, in every sentence, you trace the hand, or the obvious influence of the hand, that penned *Getting Married*. Let it be added that the writer is as genially intolerant of George Bernard Shaw as he is of the critics who venture to speak disrespectfully of the products of that master mind. *Fanny's First Play* is a play within a play. [*There follows a brief plot summary of the main play.*] The play [within], however, is the thing which occupies the greater part of the evening. For at least one act you will guess vainly what it is all about. But gradually it begins to take hold upon the spectator, and as the author's purpose slowly reveals itself the absurdity of the whole affair proves irresistible. Scrutinised from one point it is just everyday melodrama of the most conventional pattern; then again come flashes of pure Ibsenism; but in the end there is no possible conclusion save that the piece is a wilful blend of Shavian philosophy and Shavian eccentricity. The writer does not even spare us the long and tedious "discussions," which begin anywhere and lead nowhere, and which, notwithstanding, are as closely packed with wit and mental vivacity and observation as an egg is of meat. During the last act the company sit around the tea-table and fire off their verbal squibs after the fashion which we know so well and have learned to associate with the name of one dramatist only. Last night Mr Shaw, from the depths of a private box, followed the course of the play with an air of an interested spectator, whose enjoyment is not in any way marred by a fore-knowledge of what is to come. But that, doubtless, was merely part of the elaborate joke.

The plot is agreeably topsy-turvey and illogical. [*There follows a brief plot description.*] "From grave to gay, from lively to severe," the conversation ranges over a limitless area; the ball no sooner slips from the fingers of one person than it is caught up by another and thrown into the air. Manifestly there is no valid reason why the debate should ever come to an end, save that the curtain must fall at some time and so bring it to a conclusion more or less premature.

By way of epilogue, the author of *Fanny's First Play* re-assembles his forces, with the object of affording the critics an opportunity of airing their views. Here, again, the fooling is of excellent quality and quite legitimate. The performers, too, rise fully to the occasion. Mr Claude King as Trotter, Mr S.

Creagh Henry as Vaughan, Mr Reginald Owen as Gunn, and Mr Nigel Playfair as Bannel could scarcely be bettered. Nor are the honours of the skit itself less worthily upheld by Miss Lillah McCarthy as Margaret Knox, Miss Cicely Hamilton as Mrs Knox (a singularly beautiful impersonation), Miss Gwenneth Galton as Mrs Gilbey, Mr Fewlass Llewellyn as her husband, Mr Shiel Barry as Bobby, Miss Dorothy Minto as Dora, and Mr H.K. Ayliff as Juggins, the ducal man-servant. For the admirable work done by Mr Harcourt Williams as Count O'Dowda, Miss Christine Silver as his daughter, and Mr Raymond Lanserte as Lieutenant Duvallet, a good word must also be spared.

How He Lied to Her Husband
Palace Theatre, 4 December 1911
Daily Telegraph, 5 December 1911

If anyone ever doubted that the wit of Mr Bernard Shaw would feel at home in the middle of variety entertainment, that obtuse person was discomfited last night. [*How He Lied to Her Husband* is an] exhilarating trifle ... free from any of Mr Shaw's impulses to be sage.... The audience seemed to enjoy it all heartily, though one would not like to swear that many of them had a very clear idea of what all the fuss about Candida meant. But, of course, there is no reason why that should stop anyone laughing, and it did not.... You will hardly find a wittier half-hour in London.

Androcles and the Lion
St James's Theatre, 1 September 1913
Daily Telegraph, 2 September 1913

Some pantomime fun of the best. Plenty of wit, which was never quite as good, but, for the most part, good enough. Two or, perhaps, three characters who did not mind being real. A modicum of rhetoric on the whole duty of man. Some fascinating groups and backgrounds, with the modes and robes of Imperial Rome, much more graceful and harmonious than we have any reason to believe they were. Such is Mr Bernard Shaw's new play, *Androcles and the Lion*.

Everybody since Aulus Sellius [sic: Gellius]—or whoever it was that invented the tale—knows of Androcles and the lion whom he relieved of a thorn, the grateful lion who in due season declined to dine upon his surgeon. From this we used to learn when we were children and morals were simpler to be kind to animals. Of course, Mr Bernard Shaw does not forget that lesson. His homiletics contain several agreeable passages on the subject. But chiefly he uses his "fable play" to talk about the vocation of the martyr and the proper limits of obedience to the stale and even the dim ultimate realties of religious hope and faith. Some fine touches of character emerge, some interesting changes and problems of conduct in peril of death. And all this is mixed up with simple obvious fun about a nagging wife and the dietetic value of the early Christian and the delightful antics of the quaintest of sham lions. It is a queer mixture, and if almost all of it is interesting there are uncomfortable moments. Even while we laughed we had some qualms of conscience. There is no great harm, indeed, in a joke or two over the horrors of two thousand years since. So long as we do not allow our laughter to mix with any thought of the reality. But when a dramatist has been using all the resources of his art to make us imagine what manner of women they were who would rather be torn by beasts before the brutalised mob of Rome than sham a moment's service to the old gods, we are not free to laugh the next instant at the oddity of a too human lion. The noble company of martyrs spoil for us the fun of Boxing Night.

EARLY CHRISTIANS

Perhaps a pure historical sense would remark that Mr Shaw's early Christians are not really two thousand years old, or two thousand days. There is some truth in that, but less than you would expect. They are indeed more real than most of Mr Shaw's adventures into history. Perhaps, because the Christian who died in the arena before Nero or Domitian was more of our world than his own. Two of these people, at least, are real enough to impose themselves on your thought. Androcles the meek and Ferrovius the muscular Christian. Androcles is the man born always to turn the other cheek, long suffering, and of infinite kindness. Our slang would call him a humanitarian. The sufferings of animals hurt him more than his own. The only thing which ever roused him to violence was a man's cruelty to a beast. You begin to think of St Francis:

> He that in his Catholic wholeness used to call the very flowers
> Sisters, brothers. And the beasts, whose pains are hardly less than ours.

Like John Wesley and older saints, he cannot admit that the dumb animals have no souls. But he loves humanity all the more, and his character, not much in Mr Shaw's usual manner, is more than enough to save the play. If you object that there is not much of distinctively Christian faith about him, it is true but irrelevant. He is a Christian born, not made, a Christian not by dogma, but after the spirit. He belongs to the school of

> I turned my cheek to the smiter precisely as Scripture says,
> And, following that, I knocked him down and led him up to grace.

He would not, indeed, accept that doctrine. His chief fear is being roused to smite, and his consummation is a great killing in the arena. But his habit is to deal with the unbeliever doughtily, and thereby he makes many converts. He is drawn in rather rough outline, with rather bold colour, but there is no doubt of his reality, and perhaps with his simple fear of his own strength he is the most true to his period of all the company. There is another, Spintho, a rascal turned Christian merely for the sake of Heaven, finely hit off in a few strokes, but he is only a sketch.

The elaborate Lavinia is far less convincing. To her is given a defence of the Christian obstinacy and of the duty of martyrdom, which rings true enough to 1913, but seemed to bear little resemblance to anything a Christian martyr of the second century would have said. We were, indeed, never deluded into the belief that she was a Christian at all. She was obviously a noble and high-minded girl. But she did not appear to have any religious faith to which the tolerant Roman Empire would have objected. She would burn no incense to the old gods. But if we understood her, she would have joined heartily with St Paul's Athenians in erecting an altar to the Unknown. It was not for that that the people who called themselves Christians went to their death. In her case, at least, it seems to have escaped Mr Shaw's notice that a Christian believes in Christ. She is, in fact, a clever young woman of our own much debating, much doubting, much speculating century, not of the great clash between paganism and another faith.

A BRIEF TALE

[A plot summary follows.]

All this was put on the stage very effectively by Mr Albert Rothenstein. We did not care for the quaint post-impressionist forest in which Androcles met his lion, but the arena before the scenes and behind was a notable piece of work, and the costumes in design and colour and grouping were delightful. Merely as a spectacle the play was a triumph for Mr Rothenstein and Mr Granville Barker [director]. The chief opportunities of acting fell to Mr O.P. Heggie as Androcles and Mr Alfred Brydone as Ferrovius. Mr Heggie, while missing none of the fun, contrived to give us a character of delicacy and charm. There was a rare beauty in some of his scenes, and always he made the quaint fellow a real and human man. Mr Alfred Brydone had broader and simpler effects to make and succeeded perfectly. It was a sound and robust piece of work, altogether true to life. Miss Lillah McCarthy looked magnificent as the patrician Christian Lavinia, and spoke the many fine things she had to say with an admirable grace. Mr Ben Webster was a noble tribune of the legion, and Mr Leon Quartermaine made the most of the fun given to the Emperor. We must not forget Mr Edward Sillward's Lion, probably the most popular character in the play, a purely delicious beast, with the most alluring pussy cat antics.

Pygmalion
His Majesty's Theatre, 11 April 1914
Daily Telegraph, 13 April 1914

ROMANCE IN FIVE ACTS

Here is Mr Shaw in his most benign mood. He could not here find it in his heart to give anything sharper than a genial thrust at his dearest enemies. For once, he lets off with a caution even the middle-classes, even morality. It would have been too great a sacrifice not to bring them into court. The hero is permitted to assure us without a glimpse of irony visible that a sneer spoils the look both of the face and the soul.

That sweet sentiment you certainly never expected to find taking itself seriously in a play of Mr Shaw's. But if he has eliminated the mordancy from his fun, it remains famous good stuff, and it is generously scattered over most of the five acts of *Pygmalion*. When Sir Herbert Tree made a little speech at the fall of the curtain he explained that there had been so much laughter that Mr Shaw had left the theatre in despair. But he must needs be a very superior person who could receive *Pygmalion* in reverent silence. It is, indeed, an ambitious enterprise to write a farce in five acts, and Mr Shaw's success is not quite complete. He lapsed into some longueurs, and one of them, which fell unfortunately at the end, was very long. But the play, as a whole, is a joyful piece of work. There is abundant vigour in it, and the best things come with such force, and the worst have so much spirit, and the thing marches on with such gaiety that you cannot resist it, nor do you want to. It is a great joke, and it comes off.

ROMANCE AND DISCUSSION

You observe that Mr Shaw calls it not a farce, but a romance. He may decline to admit any difference. Farces, indeed, are of a thousand and one species, and if you must define *Pygmalion* precisely, you might call it a farce discussionary. It debates and dallies with all sorts of solemn subjects in the midst of its fun. It suggests all sorts of problems, problems of our social state, of ethics, of human nature, even of scholarship, and, having suggested them, drops them and goes gaily on. So much of it is more like the careless, haphazard talk of two or three clever people after dinner than any other creation of the human intellect. You never get anywhere, you do not much want to get anywhere, but you meet plenty of good things on the way. Now you hear something about divisions of classes, now a scrap about heredity and environment, now a jibe or two at culture, now a little fun with conventional morality and the natural man. You must never follow anything up, you glance off from one to the other extremity of human interests, and when the evening is done you feel that you have had a great deal of good talk.

This should not suggest that *Pygmalion* does not belong to the theatre. Half the flavour would be out of it as a play to read. It has any number of scenes, which go most gaily upon the stage, and one or two which flash out brilliantly. But it is sheer farce. You are not troubled with any illusions about the reality of these funny people. Once or twice they may raise questions as to what they are at or what Mr Shaw meant by them. But the play sails gaily on, and you never suppose that such questions matter. There is just enough suggestion or caricature of character to hold your interest, and the scheme of things would be top-heavy if there were more. One rather elaborate portrait, a dustman who proudly proclaims himself one of the Undeserving Poor, and holds that the trade of being such is the only one with any "ginger in it," makes a profession of solid reality. He is in a sense real. He is a possible and a hugely amusing attitude to life. But he reveals himself in the manner of an essay on his views, spoken, of course, in the right dialect, rather than in the way the real man would talk and act. He is, in fact, a character described, not created. He has seldom made it more amusing than in Alfred Doolittle.

THE STORY

The story can be put into a sentence or two. [*Many more than two sentences are then devoted to outlining the plot, act by act. The arrival of Doolittle in act two provided "the best fun of the evening"—until act three.*]

THE SANGUINARY ADJECTIVE

Mr Doolittle was a joy. But as a piece of stage effect the fun of the next act was more brilliant still. Eliza's education had progressed. Pygmalion Higgins took her to call on his mother. She spoke with the most beautiful accent, when the machinery started. It took some time, to be sure, especially over the aspirates. But it was very beautiful. What she said was otherwise. The culture had not dealt with her grammar or her choice of subject. So we had Mrs Patrick Campbell's most dulcet tones, first talking of the weather in the language of the Meteorological Office, then murmuring of gin, and then cooing forth the story of an aunt who died ultimately because someone "done it on her," and the incongruity was very delectable. There was a good deal of it all, excellent stuff, ending with an irresistible climax. Eliza was going. Now even as a girl of the grove Eliza loved the taxicab. Would Eliza the cultured walk? Then in her sweetest tones, "Walk?" said she. "Not b— likely!" That brought down the house.

[*In concluding his plot summary, the review reflects on the relationship between Higgins and Eliza.*]

What did they think of each other? This Pygmalion did not "find the statue warm." She was a shrewish young person, even in fine feathers and a fine accent. He loudly proclaimed his indifference to women. She ran away, but she ran to his mother's house. What was to become of her? Was the transformation more than superficial? When she saw her father again—poor Mr Doolittle made rich for other folk to "touch," about to be respectable and already resplendent—she relapsed into a cockney giggle. But afterwards she scolded Higgins as capably as any other of Mr Shaw's young women. We fancied that the strange ménage was going on after the curtain fell, but we did not care a straw, for there was nothing in these people but matter for laughter, and we had laughed enough, and the curtain kept us waiting too long.

BRILLIANT ACTING

Save for a lack of speed, the performance was brilliant. When some scenes go more quickly the acting will be as near perfection as anything in this world. Mrs Patrick Campbell disguised herself excellently in the flower girl's primitive squalor, and her cockney accent was (to one who cannot distinguish a hundred and thirty vowel sounds) exactly right and supremely funny. The whole attitude of the girl was excellently managed. With very delicate art we had the gradual progress of Eliza suggested, and throughout the scene in which the small talk of the gutter comes with slow, elaborate beauty, Mrs Campbell's comedy was rich and rare. Afterwards, as a fine lady, she played with any amount of fire. Sir Herbert Tree, as Higgins, has a part in which his wit and his power of inventing by-play have full scope, and he used them to delightful purpose. There were a thousand and one little touches of oddity, all perfectly right and vividly expressive. We may wonder whether Mr Shaw meant Higgins to be rather more of a brute than Sir Herbert Tree suggests, but if he were, other parts of the character would be puzzling. Sir Herbert's Higgins is a most genially comic realisation of a man uniting Wellington's distinctions in one, "I have no small talk and Peel has no manners," and behind all that the oddity and the intellectual authority with which we devoutly credit our professors. There was a triumph of fun in Mr Edmund Gurney's Doolittle, a new species of "golden dustman." He put the richest unctuous humour into the admirable rogue and his quaint antics, his manner, his bearing were the jolliest stuff. Just to hear him troll out "undeserving poor" and "middle-class morality" was to yield to laughter. There was some sound work by Mr Philip Merivale as the phonetic colonel, a most natural study of middle age, and Miss Geraldine Olliffe as the professor's housekeeper. The laughter and applause were loud, but rather less towards the end.

Heartbreak House
Royal Court Theatre, 18 October 1921
Daily Telegraph, 19 October 1921
[Reprinted in part in Evans 246-48]

There are two ways of considering a play by Mr Bernard Shaw: (1) as a thing complete in itself and rounded off to a perfect end; or (2) in the light of a pendant to the explanatory preface which it is his custom to provide for the edification of readers. The second method has the disadvantage of suggesting an assumed superiority over the ordinary theatre-goer who, through want of opportunity or lack of ability to furnish forth the needful sum to obtain a copy of the published piece, comes to a performance forced to grapple, as best he may, with the subtleties and intricacies of the author's style. What precise moral he drew from last night's production of *Heartbreak House* at the Court it would be interesting to discover. Possibly after witnessing the extraordinary behaviour of the various characters in the first two acts he would accept Hector Hushabye's dictum that "one of two things must happen. Either out of the darkness some new creation will come to supplant us as we have supplanted the animals, or the heavens will fall in thunder and destroy us." Or, distrusting that gentleman's sincerity, as he had every reason to do, he might agree with Ellie Dunn that "there's nothing real in the world except my father and Shakespeare. Marcus's tigers are false; Mr Mangan's millions are false; there is nothing really strong and true about Hesione but her beautiful black hair; and Lady Utterword's is too pretty to be real." Alas! she is not the first, or likely to be the last, to discover that this world we live in is a world of illusions, and woe betide her or him who is compelled to stand aside and silently see them subjected to an agonising process of disintegration. It takes Mr Shaw a portentously long time to arrive at either of these conclusions. His loquacity grows with the passing years, although happily his wit shows little sign of dimming brilliancy. True, there are in *Heartbreak House* lengthy sketches during which the interest is apt to dwindle, for the characters will be talking when they should be up and doing. With hardly an exception they bear, also, the true Shavian brand. They are the most elusive and contradictory creatures in the world. At one moment they are all sympathy and conciliation; at another they are fighting like cat and dog. One might expect that their creator would have some mercy upon them; but no, he merely uses them as puppets upon which to exercise his utmost diabolical skill as a marksman. At the beginning his heroine, Ellie Dunn, is the model of a timid, impressionable young English girl, only to develop a few hours later into a cold, pitiless, calculating woman. Captain Shotover, the patriarch of the family, is a hard-swearing, domineering, tetchy old man in whom, to your surprise, you suddenly discover there is a genuine vein of romance and gentleness. Boss Mangan, the apparently strong man of the party, unexpectedly reveals himself as a feeble trickster, who had not even the ability to feather his own nest. And so the tale goes on until you begin to ask yourself, "Is life, in this the twentieth century, bereft of all sense of honesty, of true feeling, or of honour?"

Time, unfortunately, does not permit of any detailed account of last night's performance. The blame must be laid to the charge of the author, whose piece occupied full four hours in representation, and to the fact that the Court Theatre stands at some considerable distance from Fleet-street. Better acting, however, it would be difficult to point to. Miss Ellen O'Malley's study of Ellie Dunn was a wonderfully finished piece of work, conspicuous for its clever exposition of the curiously contrasted phases of the character. Mr Brember Wills has given us nothing so good as his splendidly balanced and thoroughly effective portrait of Captain Shotover, while as Lady Utterword Miss Edith Evans was at last permitted to show herself as a marvellously fascinating, clever, and beautiful woman. Nor could the Hector Hushabye of Mr James Dale have been improved on; in him were combined the qualities not only of the affected dandy, but of the irresistible dompteur de femmes [*tamer of women*]. As Boss Mangan Mr Alfred Clark added one more inimitable specimen to his gallery of life-like portraits. Particularly good work was done also by Mr Charles Grove as the Burglar, a singularly neat thumb-nail sketch by Mr Eric Maturin as Randall Utterword, and Miss Lilian Talbot as Nurse Guinness. In Mrs Hushabye Miss Mary Grey found a part admirably suited to her personality, and played it with fine judgment and excellent discretion.

Back to Methuselah

Part I: *In the Beginning*
Royal Court Theatre, 18 February 1924
Daily Telegraph, 19 February 1924

It was like the famous nights of twenty years ago to find the Court Theatre last evening crowded for the first London performance of a Shaw play, with distinguished people everywhere, and all the old enthusiasm. The first section of *Back to Methuselah* is not perhaps altogether its happiest. With Adam, Eve, the Serpent, and Cain as its characters, it is more remote from "the businesses and bosoms of men" than your average playgoer may care for. Last evening's audience, however, followed its conversation—and it is little more—with rapt attention, and evidently enjoyed it to the full. Obviously this could mean only one thing, namely, that there must have been a deal of wholly admirable speaking, and here, indeed, the interpreters may be congratulated. In the scene in Paradise Mr Colin Keith Johnston both spoke and bore himself remarkably well as our first father. He has a good voice and managed its inflections without apparent effort. In the difficult part of the Serpent Miss Caroline Keith also greatly impressed the house, and brought out every scrap of meaning in the fiend's share of the dialogue. Miss Gwen Ffrangcon-Davies's Eve in this scene pleased us less; it seemed artificial and strained; but in the ensuing Mesopotamia episode, where the mother of us all is 300 years old, the actress seemed more at her ease, and one of the treats of the evening was her delivery of the fine passage in which the future coming of the poet, the musician, and the sculptor is foreshadowed. The poet, by the way, would appear to be of the "minor" order, with a touch in him of the Conscientious Objector—but it is a fine speech as a whole, and Miss Ffrangcon-Davies gave it beautifully. Mr Scott Sunderland as a handsome and resonant "first murderer" completed the cast. To-night we are to have the more familiar Shaw in the up-to-date scene dealing with the Brothers Barnabas, and laughter should reign supreme.

Part II: *The Gospel of the Brothers Barnabas*
Royal Court Theatre, 19 February 1924
Daily Telegraph, 20 February 1924

Another crowded audience gathered in the Court Theatre last evening for the second part of the Shavian Pentateuch, *Back to Methuselah*, and sat for two hours drinking in the scientific arguments and revelations of the two Barnabas Brothers, and the mutual recriminations of the Liberal leaders,

Lubin and Joyce Burge, in other words, Mr Asquith and Mr Lloyd George. As everyone knows, the episode ends with the revelation that, by force of will, a man may extend his life-span from 70 to 300 years. Mr Shaw does not go at all deeply into the matter. For example, he ignores that conflict with the pull of the earth which every mortal is unconsciously waging by day and night, awake and asleep, and which in the end would kill him even if there were nothing else to bring about death. But it is all very gay, and unusual, and antinomian, and the audience enjoyed the talk of the little group of almost motionless characters quite as much as other audiences elsewhere were enjoying plays in which all the laws of dramatic construction were faithfully observed. The performance as a whole was not quite satisfactory. Dialogue cut into such formidable lengths, and so entirely unlike that of the ordinary play, cannot be easy to memorise, and the impersonators of the two political protagonists (in all other respects admirable) [Leo Carroll as Joyce Burge, and Osmund Willson as Lubin] were repeatedly feeling their way to their words, a handicap which will no doubt diminish with the promised repetitions of the cycle. The two Barnabases, however, were extremely well done by Mr Wallace Evennett and Mr Frank Moore, and the clear speech of the latter was particularly welcome. Miss Eileen Beldon, as Savvy, was a little indistinct of speech, but threw plenty of fire into her part when the opportunity offered; and the minor parts of the clergyman and the parlourmaid were in safe hands [Cedric Hardwicke and Margaret Chatwin]. The scene, a Hampstead drawing room, was picturesquely arranged, and if the prospect from the windows bore little resemblance to any part of Hampstead-heath, it made an effective stage picture. There was great enthusiasm at the end.

Part III: *The Thing Happens*
Royal Court Theatre, 20 February 1924
Daily Telegraph, 21 February 1924

Confucius, the British Chief Secretary; the British Islands' negress Health Minister; the President of those islands (for it is 2170 A.D., and England is no longer Tennyson's "crowned republic"), and other characters in the third section of Mr Shaw's Pentateuch, proved last evening, at the Court Theatre, much livelier company than the Liberal leaders had been the night before. For one thing we knew those leaders long before Mr Shaw started having his fun at their expense. For another, the actors last night knew their parts; and one of the characters, that of the Archbishop of York, who has lived through four drownings to be over 270 years old, and to look and sound like a handsome 50, was quite beautifully spoken by Mr Cedric Hardwicke, who gave us the further impression that it would have been as beautifully acted if there had been anything to act. But of course there is nothing. It is a case of voces et preterea nihil [voices and nothing else]. Characters come in, sit down, talk, go out, and, as they say in America, that is all there is "to it." Nevertheless, the thing holds the audience, for it is full of ideas, some old, some new, all amusing; and at the end comes the dramatic touch that the 300-years-span of life is a fact, and that the story of humanity has made a fresh start. Nobody in the audience believes in it. The whole thing is only a fairy-tale; but the wit and novelty of it bubble gaily, and there is one uncanny, creepy moment in which the 260-years-old Domestic Minister, Mrs Lutestring, asks the doubting President of the Islands to look at her face and believe in her antiquity, and he obeys, and presently in horror recoils and hides his own. Mr Terence O'Brien as the President, and Mr Paul Smythe as the Chinaman filled their respective roles with British bonhomie and Oriental inscrutability; and when at last the curtain fell the whole company were called and applauded to the echo by an audience that once more filled the house.

Part IV: *The Tragedy of an Elderly Gentleman*
Royal Court Theatre, 21 February 1924
Daily Telegraph, 22 February 1924

The Shavian Pentateuch took its fourth leap at the Court Theatre last evening, and landed us on the southern shore of Galway Bay in the year 3000 A.D. By this time London has vanished. Baghdad is the capital of the British Commonwealth (and of British sport), and the only thing exported from what were called the British Isles is Wisdom! In these circumstances the British Prime Minister comes from the Tigris to Galway to consult a local Oracle as to the best date for a coming dissolution of Parliament and [a] General Election. Such is the basis on which last evening's three acts, and nearly three hours of talk, were built up; and round and round in circles it went on, settling nothing, mocking at most things, helpful to nobody, but, at any rate in its first and third acts, keeping another crowded audience vastly diverted. And once more we had some quite delightful elocution, notably from Mr Scott Sunderland, who not only delivered the long speeches of the Elderly Gentleman with the varied humour, pathos, rhetorical exuberance, and at times grandeur they demanded, but acted the part so realistically that, with all his oddities, the character seemed really alive. Miss Caroline Keith, as Fusima, made a musical and intellectual contribution to the talk, as also did Miss Eileen Beldon in the long part of Zoo; Mr Osmund Willson had at least one genuinely dramatic moment, when the Oracle (following the example of Tom Moore's "Veiled Prophet") revealed her face and sent him cowering in terror to the floor; and the minor parts were all carefully done. The scene of the Temple with its far-off Oracle enthroned beyond an abyss was well done; but the *Magic Flute* trombone-cry which was supposed to have accompanied the magic utterance, was sufficiently out of tune to make Mozart turn in his grave.

Part V: ***As Far As Thought Can Reach***
Royal Court Theatre, 22 February 1924
***Daily Telegraph*, 23 February 1924**

Mr Shaw's Biological Pentateuch reached its "fifthly and lastly" at the Court Theatre last evening. The concluding section is dated 31920 A.D., by which time not only has the British Commonwealth (even in its Baghdad phase) disappeared, but human beings, like chickens, are hatched from eggs, and when they first appear from the shell are fully grown and ready for what the gaoler in *The Yeoman of the Guard* describes as "indiscriminate caress." They also indulge in dances as "blameless" as those in the second act of *Ruddigore*—and do so to what sounds exceedingly like a gramophone accompaniment. Indeed, during the first part of last evening's entertainment the stage picture was quite Gilbertian, though the talk made heavy going. But in the second part it became a nightmare. The children—i.e., the lately hatched—in this remote period were only able to keep young and lively for four years. With the dawn of their fourth birthday they changed into Ancients, and then lived on for thousands of years, for nothing but thought; with the result that they became extremely bald and perfectly dreadful to look at. And two of these worthies, monumentally impersonated by Mr Cedric Hardwicke and Miss Caroline Keith, talked on all sorts of subjects for years and years, until the stage darkened, and Lilith appeared and brought the whole strange dream to an end. Another grim feature of this section was the behaviour of a couple of Bakstian-looking automata, or Frankenstein monsters, one of whom, a woman, killed a 3-year-old child, and then peacefully passed away (to more gramophone music) with her partner, and the two were taken out to be cremated. What can we say? The whole thing was nobly spoken, not only by those already named, but also conspicuously by Miss Frances Doble [Ecrasia], Mr Terence O'Brien [Martellus], and Mr Colin Keith Jackson [*sic*: Johnston, who played Pygmalion]; the house was packed; the author was called, but somebody told us he was not in the house; and there were all the signs that the remaining performances of the cycle will enjoy a similar measure of public curiosity. But, as Calverley remarked in one of his delightful parodies, "As to the meaning, it's what you please!"

Saint Joan
New Theatre, 26 March 1924
Daily Telegraph, 27 March 1924

It is a strange thing that though many men have put Joan of Arc into plays, no man has succeeded in making out of her career a truly memorable play until now. London—that part of the population of London, at all events, which goes to the theatre—has been strung up to the topmost pitch of anticipation for some time past at the prospect of seeing what Mr Shaw has made of the career of the Maid of Orleans; and those who were fortunate enough to be present at the first performance found their hopes fulfilled of seeing a remarkable piece of work. Not that this is a play to please everybody. Mr Shaw is Mr Shaw still, even though he is appearing in an unfamiliar guise, and even though that buried poet which we are told lurks in him is given a bigger share of the work here than in any other of his plays. Nor will everybody acquiesce in Mr Shaw's version of the story. The drama of Joan as he sees it is a drama without a villain. Peter Cauchon, Bishop of Beauvais, who condemned Joan, is no villain but a good churchman bent on saving a soul and stamping out heresy. Richard de Beauchamp, Earl of Warwick, is no villain but an early diehard convinced that in Joan's ideas of kingship lies mortal danger to the feudal system. Mr Shaw states that there is no historical evidence that Joan's judges were corrupt; he believes, indeed, the exact opposite, and points out as an anomaly that at her trial, when the merciful men by whom she was tried did everything to help her that they could reconcile with their beliefs and their consciences to do, Joan was adjudged guilty of deadly sin, and was handed over to the secular arm to be burnt; while twenty-five years later, when the trial was repeated by a thoroughly corrupt and dishonest court, Joan's memory was cleared and she appeared in her true colours. So much, says Mr Shaw, for the short-lived human being doing his best according to his lights. [*A plot summary follows.*] Let it be said at once that Mr Shaw's Joan is a very beautiful creation, and one which none but he could have drawn. She is fashioned out of two qualities, faith and simplicity; by these she succeeds, by these she fails, and by these she is at last exalted. The exaltation Mr Shaw has shown by means of an epilogue, in the form of a dream wherein the chief characters appear to the French king and discuss Joan's career and death, and the after-effects thereof. This scene shows us Mr Shaw at his old games again. It is designed to make, and does make, "a glorious ending" to the tale; yet it is a strange mixture of poetry and flippancy, wherein the author does not hesitate to go out of his way to poke a little cheap topical fun. This, however, is as much in the Shaw tradition as the figure of the Chaplain de Stogumber, the stupid Englishman whom we have seen in *Caesar and Cleopatra* and *John Bull's Other Island*, and last met in the Elderly Gentleman of *Back to Methuselah*.

MISS THORNDIKE

The part of Joan might have been written for Miss Thorndike. No actress that could have been chosen could better have hit off the Maid's simplicity without losing her strength. Her spell is slow. She does not grip the imagination entirely in the first two scenes, with the result that Joan's swift subjugation of de Baudricourt and the Dauphin seems rather an arbitrary ipse-dixit [he himself said it] on the part of the author than a recognition on their part of her divine mission. But once she does take hold she never lets her grip slacken. This is a big piece of work, done in a big way; perhaps all the bigger because there is in it no violent passion, but—what is far more difficult—a sustained ecstasy. The rest of the long cast is worth more consideration than the mere word or two which is all that time will now permit us. Mr Ernest Thesiger plays the Dauphin according to his manner, making a clever study of his weakness and folly, but hardly suggesting the contrast of his subsequent accession to a measure of manhood. Mr Eugene Leahy, as Cauchon, gives that one-idea'd churchman a fine frenzy of fanaticism which makes this the best achievement of his career so far as we have observed. Mr Lewis Casson gives a very complete sketch of Mr Shaw's Englishman [de Stogumber]; Messrs Milton Rosmer [Bluebeard], Robert Horton [Dunois], Lawrence Anderson [Ladvenu], and Lyall Swete [Warwick] all do excellent work, and Mr O.B. Clarence [the Inquisitor] [is] more than excellent. Others, such as Messrs Bruce Winston [La Trémouille], Raymond Massey [La Hire], and Shayle Gardner [de Baudricourt], are worthy of mention; and Miss Beatrice Smith must be put on record as being the only woman in the cast except Miss Thorndike who has a line to say. Even she only has one.

SOURCES

Courtney, W.L. *Old Saws and Modern Instances*. New York: E.P. Dutton, 1918.
——. *The Passing Hour*. London: Hutchinson & Co. [1925].
Davis, Tracy C. "Theatre Critics in Late Victorian and Edwardian Periodicals: A Supplementary List." *Victorian Periodicals Review* 17.4 (1984): 158-64.
Dukore, Bernard, ed. *Bernard Shaw. The Drama Observed*. 4 vols. University Park, PA: Pennsylvania State University Press, 1993.
Egan, Michael, ed. *Ibsen: The Critical Heritage*. London: Routledge & Kegan Paul, 1972.
Evans, T.F., ed. *Shaw: The Critical Heritage*. London: Routledge & Kegan Paul, 1976.
Ford, Ronald, ed. *The Letters of Bernard Shaw to* The Times *1898-1950*. Dublin: Irish Academic Press, 2007.
Gibbs A.M. *A Bernard Shaw Chronology*. Houndmills, Basingstoke: Palgrave, 2001.
Kent, Christopher. "Periodical Critics of Drama, Music, & Art, 1830-1914: A Preliminary List." *Victorian Periodicals Review* 13.1/2 (1980): 31-55.
Laurence, Dan H., ed. *Bernard Shaw: A Bibliography*. 2 vols. Oxford: Clarendon Press, 1983.
——. *Bernard Shaw: Collected Letters*. 4 vols. New York: Viking Penguin, 1985-88.
——. *Bernard Shaw Theatrics*. Toronto: University of Toronto Press, 1995.
Mander, Raymond, and Joe Mitchenson. *Theatrical Companion to Shaw*. New York: Pitman, 1955.
Nicholson, Steve. *The Censorship of British Drama 1900-1968. Volume One: 1900-1932*. Exeter: University of Exeter Press, 2003.
Nicoll, Allardyce. *A History of English Drama 1660-1900*. Volume 5, *Late Nineteenth Century Drama 1850-1900*. Cambridge: Cambridge University Press, 1967.
——. *English Drama 1900-1930. The Beginnings of the Modern Period*. Cambridge: Cambridge University Press, 1973.
Oxford Dictionary of National Biography (www.oxforddnb.com).
Shaw, Bernard. *Collected Plays with Their Prefaces*. Under the editorial supervision of Dan H. Laurence. 7 vols. London: Max Reinhardt. The Bodley Head, 1970-74.
Shaw, Bernard. *Pygmalion*. Ed. L.W. Conolly. London: Methuen, 2008.
Stephens, Russell. *The Censorship of English Drama 1824-1901*. Cambridge: Cambridge University Press, 1980.

Wearing, J.P. *American and British Theatrical Biography: A Directory.* Metuchen, N.J.: Scarecrow Press, 1979.

Wearing, J.P., ed. *The London Stage 1900-1909: A Calendar of Plays and Players.* 2 vols. Metuchen, N.J.: Scarecrow Press, 1982.

——. *The London Stage 1910-1919: A Calendar of Plays and Players.* 2 vols. Metuchen, N.J.: Scarecrow Press, 1982.

——. *The London Stage 1920-1928: A Calendar of Plays and Players.* 3 vols. Metuchen, N.J.: Scarecrow Press, 1984.

INDEX

À Beckett, Gilbert A. 28
Actors' Association 35
Actors' Orphanage Fund 11
Adelphi Theatre 68, 69
Admirable Bashville, The (Shaw) 21, 23, 24, 25, 26, 48, 75-77
Adored One, The (Barrie) 40
Afternoon Theatre, The 4, 21, 23, 26, 47, 50, 75
Ainley, Henry 24, 25, 74, 77
Ancient Mariner, The (Coleridge) 29
Anderson, Lawrence 94
Androcles and the Lion (Shaw) 5, 38, 39, 81-84
Anglo-Swedish Literary Foundation, The 47
Antony and Cleopatra (Shakespeare) 70
Apple Cart, The (Shaw) 44
Archer, William 7, 15, 46
Arms and the Man (Shaw) 18, 31, 53, 54, 80
Ashwell, Lena 38, 50, 79
Asquith, Herbert 26, 29, 90
Au Bonheur des Dames (Zola) 30, 49
Avariés, Les (Brieux) 40, 52
Ayliff, H.K. 81
Ayrton, Acton Smee 28, 49

Back to Methuselah (Shaw) 42, 89-93, 94
Bailey, Henry Christopher 3, 5
Balfour, Arthur 22, 26, 29, 47
Barker, Harley Granville 4, 11, 15, 17, 19, 22, 23, 26, 30, 31, 45, 46, 49, 55, 57, 59, 61, 66, 69, 83
Barnes, J.H. 63
Barrie, James Matthew 23, 29, 32, 38, 40, 47, 49, 50
Barry, Shiel 81

Bateman, Kate 69
Baughan, E.A. 33
Bayreuth Festspielhaus 23, 47
Beerbohm, Max 32
Beethoven, Ludwig van 19
Beldon, Eileen 90, 92
Belle Héloïse, La 71
Bendall, Ernest 3
Bessier, Rudolf 32
Beveridge, J.D. 59
Booth, William 13, 46
Brieux, Eugène 40, 51
Brooke, Sarah 59
Brookfield, Charles 32, 35, 36, 37, 50
Brough, Fanny 25, 74
Browne, Graham W. 54, 57
Bryant, Charles 79
Brydone, Alfred 83
Bulwer-Lytton, Edward 76
Butt, Alfred 37, 50
By Special Request (Watson) 2

Caesar and Cleopatra (Shaw) 3, 5, 9, 10, 11, 16, 18, 45, 62, 70-72, 94
Calthorp, Donald 79
Calvert, Louis 57, 61
Campbell, Mrs Patrick 9, 13, 27, 38, 42, 45, 46, 48, 51, 86
Candida (Shaw) 71
Cannan, Gilbert 33
Captain Brassbound's Conversion (Shaw) 10, 14, 62-63, 70
Carew, James 63
Carroll, Leo 90
Cashel Byron's Profession (Shaw) 25, 76
Casson, Lewis 94
Célimare le bien-aimé (Labiche and Delacour) 50

Chamberlain, Joseph 36, 49
Chapman and Hall 1
Chatwin, Margaret 90
Chester, Elsie 54
Chinese Lantern, The (Housman) 17, 46
Chocolate Soldier, The (Straus) 31
Civic and Dramatic Guild, The 29
Clarence, O.B. 94
Clark, Alfred 88
Clark, Holman 74
Club of First Nighters, The 39
Comedy Theatre 49
Cornwallis-West, Mrs; see Campbell, Mrs Patrick
Courtney, William Leonard 1, 3, 5
Craig, Edward Gordon 24, 48
Creighton, Mandall 19, 47
Criterion Theatre 23
Culton, Sidonie 29
Cymbeline (Shakespeare) 24, 48

Daily Express 7
Daily Mail 3
Dale, James 88
Dark Lady of the Sonnets, The (Shaw) 32
David Ballard (McEvoy) 30, 49
Davis, Fay 13
Day, Marjorie 69
Dear Old Charlie (Brookfield) 36, 50
Dearmer, Mrs Percy 36, 50
Dearmer, Percy 50
Delacour, Alfred-Charlemagne 50
Devil's Disciple, The (Shaw) 10, 16, 53, 62, 68-70, 71
Dickens, Charles 39, 51
Disraeli, Benjamin 71
Dissoluto Punito, Il 40, 51
Doble, Francis 92
Doctor's Dilemma, The (Shaw) 5, 7, 14, 15, 16, 39, 46, 51, 63-66
Don Giovani (Mozart) 51
Don Juan in Hell (Shaw) 16, 18, 66-67
Dramas and Diversions (Courtney) 1
du Maurier, Guy 27, 48
Duke of York's Theatre 4, 29, 30, 46, 47, 49, 51, 77

Earn, James 66
Edward VII 47

Elliott, Gertrude 71, 72
Emily (Mack) 47
Englishman's Home, An (du Maurier) 27, 28, 48
Evans, Edith 88
Evennett, Wallace 90

Faber, Beryl 74
Fair Arabian, The (Culton) 29
Fanny's First Play (Shaw) 32, 33, 50, 80-81
Farren, William, jun. 66, 74
Ffrangcon-Davies, Gwen 89
Filippi, Rosina 24, 25, 61
Flower, Archibald D. 43
Forbes-Robertson, Johnston 9, 10, 29, 45, 71
Ford, Audrey 54
Fortnightly Review, The 1
Frohman, Charles 4, 29, 30, 31, 49
Fulton, Charles 74

Gaiety Theatre 29
Galsworthy, John 15, 29, 46
Galton, Gwenneth 81
Gardner, Shayle 94
Garrick Theatre 46
George, A.E. 57
German Reed Company, The 2
Getting Married (Shaw) 5, 16, 18, 20, 21, 72-75, 80
Ghosts (Ibsen) 40
Gilbert, William Schwenck 28, 38, 50, 92
Gladstone, William 28, 49
Globe Theatre 48, 51
Godwin, E.W. 48
Goodhart, Charles 59
Gore, Charles 47
Greet, Clare 66
Grey, Mary 88
Grove, Charles 88
Gurney, Edmund 63, 87
Gwenn, Edmund 59, 61, 63

Haddon, Archibald 7
Hall, K.E. 49
Halstan, Margaret 37, 50
Hamilton, Cicely 81

Hamilton, Lady Emma 13, 45
Hamlet (Shakespeare) 25
Hannele (Hauptmann) 23, 47
Happy Land, The (Gilbert and À
  Beckett) 28, 29, 49
Harben, Hubert 61, 79
Hardwicke, Cedric 90, 91, 92
Harrison, Frederick 17, 18
Hauptmann, Gerhart 23, 26, 47
Have You Seen the Shah? (see *Shah, The*)
Haydon, Florence 59, 78, 79
Haymarket Theatre 16, 20, 32, 46, 72
Hearn, James 24, 25, 74, 77
Heartbreak House (Shaw) 5, 42, 87-88
Hebbel Theatre, Berlin 49
Heggie, O.P. 79, 83
Henry, S. Creagh 81
His Borrowed Plumes (Cornwallis-West)
  48
His Majesty's Theatre 4, 21, 22, 23, 38,
  39, 47, 48, 50, 75, 84
Hobbes, Halliwell 25
Horton, Robert 94
Housman, Laurence 17
How He Lied to Her Husband (Shaw) 35,
  38, 81

Ibsen, Henrik 16, 23, 40
Imperial Institute 36, 50
Imperial Theatre 24, 48, 49
Irving, Henry 1, 24, 48
Ixion (Disraeli) 71

Jessica's First Prayer (Stretton) 15
John Bull's Other Island (Shaw) 5, 11, 12,
  18, 25, 47, 55-57, 59, 65, 66, 71, 94
Johnston, Colin Keith 89, 92
Jones, Henry Arthur 38, 46
Josephine (Barrie) 29
Joyce, Jeremiah 16, 46
Julius Caesar (Shakespeare) 10
Justice (Galsworthy) 29

Keith, Caroline 89, 91, 92
Kennedy, C. Rann 69
Kerr, Frederick 63
King, Claude 80
Kingston, Gertrude 27, 32, 48
Kingsway Theatre 29, 33

Kit Marlowe (Courtney) 1
Kitchener, Herbert 26

La Serre, Edward 2
Labiche, Eugène 50
Lady of Lyons, The (Bulwer-Lytton) 76
Lang Matheson 69
Lanserte, Raymond 81
Leahy, Eugene 94
Lee, Auriol 74
Lewes, Miriam 79
Lewis, Eric 66
Lewis, Mabel Terry 54
Little Theatre 32, 49, 80
Llewellyn, Fewlass 81
Lloyd, Frederick 79
Lloyd George, David 33, 90
Lodge, Oliver 22, 47
Löhr, Marie 24, 25, 74, 77
London Pavilion 19, 47
London Society for Women's Suffrage,
  The 26
Loraine, Robert 67, 74
Lowe, Robert 28, 49
Lowne, C.M 79
Lyceum Theatre 45, 48
Lyric Theatre 31

Macbeth (Shakespeare) 9
McCarthy, Lillah 32, 33, 49, 59, 66, 67,
  81, 84
McEvoy, Charles 30, 49
Mack, Margaret 23, 26, 47
McKinnel, Norman 67
Madras House, The (Barker) 30, 46, 49
Magic Flute, The (Mozart) 92
Major Barbara (Shaw) 4, 5, 12, 13, 14,
  25, 50, 59-61
Malvern Festival 44
Man and Superman (Shaw) 11, 25, 57-
  59, 63, 65, 66
Man of Destiny (Shaw) 16, 66
Mary Queen of Scots 13, 45
Massey, Raymond 94
Maturin, Eric 88
Merivale, Bernard 51
Merivale, Philip 87
Milner, Alfred 26
Milward, Dawson 37, 50

Minto, Dorothy 81
Misalliance (Shaw) 5, 29, 30, 38, 49, 50, 77-79
Moore, Frank 90
Moore, Tom 92
Morgan, John Pierpont 22, 47
Mozart, Wolfgang Amadeus 18, 51, 92
Mrs Warren's Profession (Shaw) 31, 35, 45, 47, 49
Murray, Gilbert 61
Musgrave, Kenyon 69
My Lady of Orange (Bailey) 3

New Amsterdam Theatre, New York 11, 45
New Theatre 46, 94
Night Hawk, The (Worrall and Merivale) 39
Notorious Mrs Ebbsmith, The (Pinero) 45

O'Brien, Terence 91, 92
Old Saws and Modern Instances (Courtney) 1
Olliffe, Geraldine 87
O'Malley, Ellen 57, 88
Orphée aux Enfers (Offenbach) 71
Owen, Reginald 81

Palace Theatre 35, 37, 38, 50, 81
Palais Royal 36, 50
Pantzer, Lina 38
Passion, Poison, and Petrifaction (Shaw) 11
Paston, George 26, 48, 75
Pawle, Lennox 25, 77
Pélissier, H.G. 27, 48
Peter Pan (Barrie) 47
Pharisee, The (Watson) 2
Pharos Club 48
Philanderer, The (Shaw) 16, 45
Pickwick Papers (Dickens) 39, 51, 75
Pilling, William 25
Pinero, Arthur Wing 13, 45, 47
Playfair, Nigel 81
Playgoers' Club, The 39
Plays Unpleasant (Shaw) 13, 45
Press Cuttings (Shaw) 26, 27, 28, 29, 48
Prince of Wales Theatre 48, 50

Prunella (Housman) 17, 46
Pygmalion (Shaw) 4, 5, 38, 39, 40, 41, 42, 51, 84-87

Quartermaine, Charles 25
Quartermaine, Leon 84
Queen's Hall 19, 47
Queen's Theatre 17

Raiemond, George 54
Rankin, Cremlin 63
Redford, George Alexander 27, 35, 48
Referee, The 32
Rhodes, Percy 72
Richard II (Shakespeare) 37, 50
Ricketts, Charles 18, 46
Robertson, Ian 72
Rorke, Mary 74
Rosmer, Milton 94
Rothenstein, Albert 83
Royal Academy of Dramatic Art 43
Royal Aquarium and Winter Garden 48
Royal Botanical Gardens 11
Royal Court Theatre 4, 11, 12, 14, 15, 16, 17, 18, 22, 23, 26, 28, 29, 45, 46, 47, 48, 49, 50, 55, 57, 59, 62, 63, 66, 70, 87, 89, 90, 91, 92
Royce, Edward William 49
Ruddigore (Gilbert and Sullivan) 92
Russell, Annie 61

Saint Joan (Shaw) 5, 42, 46, 93-94
St James's Gazette, The 2, 3
St James's Theatre 45, 47, 51, 81
Sass, Edward 25, 75
Saturday Review, The 48
Savoy Theatre 11, 16, 17, 45, 46, 68, 70
Scientific Dialogues (Joyce) 16, 46
Scott, Clement 1, 2, 3, 5, 16
Second Mrs Tanqueray, The (Pinero) 45
Shaftesbury Theatre 1, 2
Shah, The (Hall) 28, 49
Shakespeare Memorial National Theatre 32, 42
Shakespeare, William 10, 21, 24, 25, 26, 37, 42, 50, 70
Shaw, Charlotte 45
Sheerluck Jones (Watson) 2
Sherbrooke, Michael 67

Shewing-up of Blanco Posnet, The (Shaw) 50
Shine, J.L. 57
Shine, Wilfred 57
Sillward, Edward 84
Silver Box, The (Galsworthy) 15, 46
Silver, Christine 81
Smith, Aubrey 25
Smith, Beatrice 94
Smythe, Paul 91
Soutar, Farren 25
Spencer, Charles Robert 48
Stage Society, The 22, 47, 48
Statesman's Year-Book, The 19
Statistical Abstract, The 19
Stephens, York 53, 54
Stier, Theodore 18
Strand Theatre 2, 53
Straus, Oscar 31
Strauss, Richard 39
Stretton, Hesba 15, 46
Strindberg, August 23, 47
Sunday Telegraph, The 7
Sunderland, Scott 89, 91
Sutro, Alfred 38, 50
Swete, Lyall 94
Symonds, Emily Morse 48

Talbot, Lilian 88
Terris, William 69
Terry, Ellen 48, 62, 63
Terry's Theatre 2
Théâtre Intime 23
Thesiger, Ernest 94
Thomas, Agnes 57
Thorndike, Sybil 94
Three Plays for Puritans (Shaw) 10, 62
Thunderbolt, The (Pinero) 23, 47
Tilda's New Hat (Paston) 26, 48, 75
Tivoli Theatre 19, 47
Tree, Herbert Beerbohm 4, 21, 22, 35, 37, 51, 86, 87
Tribune, The 46
Twelve-Pound Look, The (Barrie) 49

Vallentin, Hugo 41
Vaudeville Theatre 50
Vedrenne, John 4, 11, 12, 15, 16, 17, 19, 22, 23, 26, 45
Vexin, Hermann 54

Wagner, Richard 23, 39, 47
Walkley, A.B. 33
Warley, Miss 11, 12
Watson, Henrietta 25
Webb, Beatrice 51
Webb, Sidney 19, 47, 51
Webster, Ben 24, 25, 26, 48, 64, 75, 76, 84
Welch, James 53, 54
Wesley, John 82
Whelen, Frederick 22, 47
Whitaker's Almanac 19
Widowers' Houses (Shaw) 7, 45, 53, 54
Wilberforce, Albert 22, 47
Wilde, Oscar 46
Williams, Harcourt 37, 50, 81
Wills, Brember 88
Willson, Osmund 90, 92
Winston, Bruce 94
Women's Suffrage Society, The 29
World, The 1
Worrall, Lechmere 51
Wyes, William 25
Wyndham's Theatre 48
Wynne-Matthison, E. 61, 69

Yeoman of the Guard (Gilbert and Sullivan) 92
Yorke, Oswald 61
You Never Can Tell (Shaw) 5, 50, 53-55

Zola, Émile 30, 49

www.ingramcontent.com/pod-product-compliance
Lightning Source LLC
Chambersburg PA
CBHW030912080526
44589CB00010B/271